A KNYGHT THERE WAS

A KNYGHT THERE WAS

The Evolution of the Knight in Literature

CHARLES MOORMAN

UNIVERSITY OF KENTUCKY PRESS
LEXINGTON, 1967

Manufactured in the United States of America
Library of Congress Catalog Card No. 67-17846

ACKNOWLEDGMENTS

FOR THEIR permission to quote copyrighted materials, I should like to thank the Oxford University Press (*The Poetical Works of Edmund Spenser*); the Clarendon Press (*The Works of Sir Thomas Malory*); Appleton-Century-Crofts (Theodore Banks' translation of *Sir Gawain and the Green Knight*); E. P. Dutton and Company (W. W. Comfort's translations of Chrétien in *Arthurian Romances*) and Houghton Mifflin Company (F. N. Robinson's edition of *The Complete Works of Geoffrey Chaucer*).

Portions of this study previously appeared in article form in *Mediaeval Studies*, the *South Atlantic Quarterly*, and the *Southern Quarterly*, and I am grateful to the editors of those journals for permission to reprint those materials here.

The writing of this book was made possible largely through grants from the American Council of Learned Societies and from the University of Southern Mississippi, and I should like to acknowledge here the generosity of these organizations. The idea of a book on the literary knight was first suggested to me by William S. Woods many years ago; it would have been a better book had he written it. The dedication is a gesture of gratitude toward and respect for a gentleman whose ability and scholarship have set a model for his faculty.

Like Erec, I am blessed with a wife "gentle and honorable, of wise speech and affable, of pleasing character and kindly mien," who like Enide has often rescued her husband in spite of himself.

C. M.

CONTENTS

INTRODUCTION

B OTH THE intent and method of this study need some
explanation. First, it should be noted that I am
not a historian and that I have not intended to
write anything resembling even a fragmentary history of
knighthood. The origins of the knight are, as the first
chapter asserts, lost in the mists and confusions of time,
and the smatterings of information that have come down
to us are not sufficient even for the professional historian,
let alone a student of literature, to fashion with any degree
of confidence into a complete statement of the early
growth of chivalry.

Nor have I attempted the usual sort of literary history,
the usual study of development and influence in which
the writers covered, whether "major" or "minor," are seen
simply as sources of information, as equal links in a chain
of evolution.

This book is thus no social or literary history but is
instead a study, literary both in intent and, I hope, in
execution, of a particular literary figure, the knight, who
first appears in the *chansons de geste*, rides triumphantly
through the great romances of the thirteenth and fourteenth centuries, appears as a philosophical pilgrim in

Chaucer, fights a heroic last-ditch stand for chivalry in the pages of Malory, becomes allegorical in Spenser, and dies away amidst the catcalls of parody, finally to be rejected by England's second poet as a figure unsuitable for epic.

Some limits need to be imposed on such a study in order to insure its coherence and point. The chronicles of knighthood are almost as numerous as the knights themselves; to discuss each of them would be to lead the reader into a maze of quests and tourneys. This volume, therefore, deals only with the major writers on chivalry and, for the most part, with those who wrote in English and who occupy important places in the English literary tradition. The reader to whom this volume is addressed is much more likely to be at home with Chaucer, Malory, and Spenser than he is with Machaut and Tasso, and while I have of necessity devoted chapters to the *Song of Roland* and to Chrétien, counterparts for which do not exist in English literature, I have for the most part relied on the works of Englishmen to chart the fortunes of the literary knight.

Nor have I in the study attempted to trace the development of the knight past the chivalric period. As the final chapter will make clear, the knight becomes in post-Renaissance literature a static literary device, capable of a variety of uses, to be sure—satire in *Don Quixote* and *Hudibras*, social commentary in Mark Twain, moralization in Tennyson—but totally disconnected with life and hence incapable of development. One could, of course, simply list the uses to which the knight figure is put in these later appearances, but since this book is intended to study the development of the knight in both literature and life, I have concluded at that point at which he becomes a figure of the past and so atrophies into a literary convention.

This book then intends three things: first, to trace the

changing concept of the character of the knight through
the really important literary works of the Middle Ages
and Renaissance, using the peripheral figures as transition
devices or as corroborative evidences of characteristics
observed in the large figures; second, to use the knight as
a means of coming to grips with the particular themes
and patterns of the major writers treated; and third, to
demonstrate, insofar as it may be demonstrated, the
significance of the knight errant and his journey in
medieval and early Renaissance literature. Because of its
implications, this last purpose needs some further explanation. It is my belief that a very strong case can be made
for the theory that the varying forms of the journey motif
may be manifestations of a single, extended metaphor
involving the recreation, in literary terms, of the quest
myth, the *rite de passage*, Toynbee's withdrawal and
return (any number of terms will do), the ritual journey
marking the transition from youthful innocence and ignorance to self knowledge, maturity, and, in religious terms,
salvation.

Such a thesis must involve to some degree that latest
of literary panaceas, the critical use of myth. But any
critical work that utilizes myth to any extent must per-
force make clear at its outset the ground rules it intends
to follow. It would seem to me that any such criticism
must rest upon two major assumptions concerning the
nature of myth: (1) that myth is in itself meaningful
(the problem of myth origin); (2) that myth is used in
literature, whether consciously or unconsciously, for a
meaningful purpose (the problem of myth transmission).
The first of these assumptions has been sufficiently
examined to have become almost self-evident; no matter
whether a critic holds to the ritual, the euhemerist, the
Jungian, or to any variation of these doctrines, he will
agree that myth is in some fashion and to some degree

meaningful. Moreover, it seems to me that the critic
has the right to hold to and use any reasonable theory of
myth origin as long as the method of critical analysis
which he raises on the structure of that theory is capable
of throwing light upon a literary text.

The second of these two assumptions, that involving
myth transmission, has a closer relationship to the problem of the function of myth in literary art. Here I would
propose a distinction. I can understand very easily the
use made of myth by modern artists who share our own
ideas, by, for example, Yeats, Auden, Eliot, and Charles
Williams. Theirs is a conscious and knowing use of myth;
when Yeats speaks of a "Ledaean body" and Eliot of the
"bloody wood," they hope by allusion to bring to a poem,
usually for the purposes of identification and comparison,
the whole context of the myth to which they refer. What
Eliot wishes us to understand in that brief allusion to the
"bloody wood" in "Sweeney among the Nightingales"
and to apply to Sweeney's situation in the tavern is not
simply the story of the ritual assassination of the priest-
king at Nemi, but of a whole complex of meaning which
is itself represented by the murder of the priest-king and
which takes on a still further relevancy when seen in
relation to the complex of meaning, or lack of meaning,
represented by Sweeney. In short, those modern writers
who use myth use it consciously, with a clearly defined
purpose.

The writers of the Middle Ages present an entirely
different problem, different not only in degree, but in
kind. Here the use of myth seems to me to be unconscious in the majority of instances. For example, we can
say that the references to figures of the Christian myth
(whether the *Gawain*-poet would, in fact, consider these
Old Testament characters "mythical" does not here affect
the point) in the following passage from *Sir Gawain and*

the Green Knight are designed to do little more than serve as ordinary metaphorical references, used here as "authorities" in typically medieval fashion to make a traditional antifeminist point about the nature of women:

> But no marvel it is for a fool to act madly,
> Through woman's wiles to be brought to woe.
> So for certain was Adam deceived by some woman,
> By several Solomon, Samson besides;
> Delilah dealt him his doom; and David
> Was duped by Bath-sheba, enduring much sorrow.[1]

But while the use of myth in this single passage is perfectly clear, can it be said that the ancient myth of initiation which underlies the poem as a whole is used consciously by the poet?[2] John Speirs states, without evidence, that it is.[3] I assert, using the same evidence, that it is not, and pending the discovery of concrete proof, I would maintain that mine is the more satisfactory point of view. Yet it is clear that the hero-quest, *rite de passage*, withdrawal-return pattern is repeated in essence, if not in detail, in *Sir Gawain and the Green Knight* and that some theory of transmission must be brought forward to explain the phenomenon.

I would here prefer to fall back upon what is traditionally called common sense rather than upon metaphysics or psychology in suggesting a possible explanation. The hero-quest, in all its tremendously varied forms, would appear to present an almost universal theme, appearing as it does over and over again in myth and in formal literature. It is not necessary, however, to be a follower of any school of myth interpretation to explain its universality. Certainly there are relatively few general literary themes which are of real importance to the human spirit. Of these, the passage of the soul through its difficulties to its triumph, *ad astra per aspera*, through the valley of the shadow of death on to the Celestial City, is constantly observable, clothed in an immense variety of forms, both in our own experience and in literature. The passage of the spirit, seen in its most articulate and naked form in the progress of the myth hero in the quest, is part of the general experience of being human. Thus, in the initiatory rites of savages, in the Holy Week of Christians, in the great myths of all peoples, this natural and omnipresent human problem and hope is elevated, by symbolic action, to universal and archetypal and, in most cases, religious heights. It seems entirely natural that this theme should appear universally. Certainly, myth provides the subconscious mind of the poet, which as Coleridge and others have demonstrated is constantly engaged in fusing disparate fragments of experience into creative wholes, with a great preformed common stock of concrete images to which all experience, however disparate, may unconsciously be referred and in terms of which it may be expressed. Thus the pattern of the hero's quest becomes the concrete vehicle, the objective correlative, by which the poet expresses his own variation of the universal quest. And in this way the poet's theme is given particularization, a local habitation and a name in literature, instead of transcription in the broad and general terms natural to philosophy but alien to art. Myth therefore becomes, if nothing else, a touchstone useful in isolating and labeling the characteristics which this universal theme inherently assumes in art and in defining the particular form, the nature of the *differentia*, which the pattern manifests in the work at hand.

In the Middle Ages the prevailing use of the allegorical rather than the symbolic method would seem to bring nearer the surface of the literary work this unconscious mythic quality which to some degree underlies all literature.[4] Myth patterns become comparatively easy to trace

in the literature of this period. Here again I would
suggest a further refinement for purpose of analysis. This
general theme of death and rebirth, initiation, withdrawal
and return appears in one dominant form in the literature
of the Middle Ages—that of the journey. Medieval literature is full of accounts of journeys: Dante travels through
the realms of the dead; travelers find their way into the
Celtic underworld; pilgrims "seken straunge strondes";
and, most important, hundreds of knights traverse hundreds of fields and forests in quest of objects strange and
high. That all of these journeys are variants of a single
basic pattern—the pattern of the archetypal journey-
initiation-quest—seems a possibility.[5] Therefore, the application of the journey myth to the specific journeys of
medieval literature would seem valuable, provided always
that the critic bear in mind that he must refrain from
identifying myth and literature, that he must not neglect
differentia once he has established *genus.* No one would
claim, of course, that such a line of action would further
illuminate *The Divine Comedy,* where the pattern is
revealed in such elevation and clarity as to render obvious
its workings and its effects.[6] But that this method of
critical analysis should throw light on the works of
Chrétien de Troyes, on *Sir Gawain and the Green Knight*
and Chaucer, on Malory and Spenser is sufficient justification for undertaking the task.

But in addition to tracing the quest myth through the
chivalric literature of the Middle Ages, this study also
presents a thesis concerning the morality of knighthood
itself: that the historical concept of chivalry presented the
knight with a contradictory code of ethics and that the
moral dilemmas into which the knight inevitably was
thrown became the central theme of "the great, the really
important literary works" of chivalry, but were almost
totally ignored by the innumerable pedestrian romances

of the period. And it is, I believe, the awareness of this conflict, and of course the genius to express it, that raises in literary importance and value the works of Chrétien above those of Froissart and *Sir Gawain and the Green Knight* above *La Mule Sanz Frain.*

These themes, the myth of knighthood and its morality, are essentially two views of the same landscape. For the quest of the hero is itself a moral journey, a testing process, a series of ethical dilemmas in which the hero must make a choice. Erec, Yvain, Lancelot, like Moses on Sinai and Christ in the Wilderness, all are tested, and the way in which each responds to his challenges not only reflects his own morality but also helps to determine the central ethic of knighthood, the myth of chivalry. In short, the closer the medieval writer comes to expressing the fundamental moral issues implicit in the chivalric code, the closer he comes to its reality, its myth.

In the development and demonstration of this twin-pronged theme of knighthood, its myth and its morality, lies whatever point this volume may have.

THE FIRST KNIGHTS

LA CHANSON DE ROLAND

ARLY in Malory's *Morte Darthur*, "the kynge sta-
blysshed all the knyghtes and gaff them rychesse
and londys; and charged them never to do outerage
nothir morthir, and allwayes to fle treson, and to gyff
mercy unto hym that askith mercy, uppon payne of
forfiture [of their] worship and lordship of kynge Arthure
for evirmore; and allwayes to do ladyes, damesels, and
jantilwomen and wydowes [socour:] strenghe hem in hir
ryghtes, and never to enforce them, uppon payne of
dethe."[1]

While a more systematic listing of knightly vows might
include a number of items omitted by Malory—principally
prowess, loyalty, and generosity—Arthur's charge to the
young knights represents the core of what the modern
reader looks back upon as the code of chivalric conduct—
honor, fair play, and respect for women, concepts very
close to the collective heart of western man. For even
though the formalized chivalric code and the knight who
exemplified it have ceased to exist as active agencies, their
influence still can be perceived, though in increasingly

fewer areas, in the daily conduct of civilized life. These concepts form the basis of the tacitly understood standard against which conduct and values at all levels of affairs are tested. It is the means by which we are able to judge the actions of both Khrushchev and Albert Schweitzer and the yardstick by which we measure the conduct of Becky Sharp in a "novel without a hero." It is the unwritten law which underlies modern man's conduct on a crowded bus or in a queue or on the *Titanic*. The chivalric code may be dismissed by any number of Angry Young Men as passé, outmoded, or Victorian, but its influence on even common daily acts can hardly be overestimated.

It is thus somewhat shocking to read contemporaneous accounts of the conduct of the real knight, even in the heyday of chivalry. Far from being the actual embodiment of Tennyson's Lancelot, he is all too often "treacherous and disobedient to [his] king, impious and profane in matters of religion, brutal and cruel in [his] dealings with common folk, and free from all respect for women."[2] Even that popular idol of chivalric conduct, Richard the Lion Hearted, apparently was guilty of atrocities at which Nazi jailers might blanch.[3] The cause of this obvious schism between our popular idea of the knight and the historic reality, between stainless gentleman and sacrilegious bully, becomes apparent in viewing the evolution of chivalry.

Both the English word "knight" and the French "chevalier" are instructive in tracing the beginnings of knighthood. The Anglo-Saxon term "cniht" at first referred to any young man, and only later in the Anglo-Saxon period did the word come to apply specifically to young noblemen who, by feudal custom, owed military service to their "eorlas." The term eventually became synonymous at times with "miles" and at times with "thegn." But in either case the "cniht" was essentially a foot soldier; the great battle poems of *Maldon* and *Brunanburh* show him standing and fighting. He was also spiritually a part of the Germanic heroic tradition, a firm part of the *comites* clustering about the court of an "eorl" to whom he owed allegiance. His opposite number in France, however, was at this time a "chevalier," a horseman, and only with the coming of the Normans to England did the armed and mounted knight of popular tradition come to that island.

Knighthood and chivalry as we generally think of them are essentially of French origin. It is unimportant whether this is due, as some commentators remark, to the warlike character of the Celts, or to their love of activity and individualism, or, more rationally, to certain Roman practices of training young members of the nobility that persisted in France through the Dark Ages. What does matter is that knighthood came into its own, from whatever origins it had sprung, with feudalism, with the creation in the eighth century of a system of defense—partly governmental, partly social, partly economic, entirely military and patriarchal. By this means the lords of Europe defended, using military indebtedness arising out of land distribution, the remnants of civilized life and, more importantly, their Christian religion, against the invasions of eastern and northern pagans—Saracens, Slavs, and Danes. The effectiveness of feudalism, itself a skillful fusing of the Roman *patrocinium* and the German *comitatus*,[4] lay in its flexibility, in its ability to fight and win its battles at the "local level," since no central government operating a single military force, no matter how powerful, could hope to defend itself against the hordes which overran Europe. Thus, the isolated and then impregnable stronghold with its tight-knit, especially trained mobile group of armor-clad defenders on horseback became the natural defense unit. And since armor and horses and weapons were costly, knighthood quickly became the prerogative and the exclusive property of the wealthy, among whom it was soon regarded as a secular religion as well as a mark of class status. By the end of the ninth century what had begun as a professional military class had become simply another division of the hereditary landed aristocracy and "the relation of suzerain and vassal, with its bonds of mutual obligation, was sanctified as the traditional organization of upper-class society."[5]

It must be understood that knighthood in the early years of the Carolingian period and in the three centuries following had not yet come to involve the chivalric virtues, other than prowess, associated with it after the Crusades. The early feudal knights were educated, but they were trained in a purely militaristic tradition. They were brave, aggressive warriors, able and usually anxious to defend their overlord and his lands, but they were closer in spirit and disposition to the warlike thegns of *Beowulf* and *Maldon* than to the courtly figures inhabiting the castles of Arthur. Prowess in arms was the chief virtue of any knight; without prowess he was of no more use than the peasant armed with a stick, and the chief admonition given him at his investiture was to be proud. The virtues of loyalty and generosity, themselves outgrowths of prowess, soon came to be valued next to prowess.[6] But since "arrogance, hatred of restraint, and love of battle were bred into the very bone of the eleventh-century French nobility,"[7] the great difficulty in the early chivalric system lay in the fact that the knight was not in any way trained for leisure. Unlike the heroes of the northern sagas who are essentially farmers and lawmakers, a knight's upbringing and social position in the feudal system freed him from responsibilities for labor. Thus, he spent his time, especially during the tenth and eleventh centuries when the dangers from without had all but disappeared, ranging about the countryside, accumulating wealth and, strangely enough, prestige, looting, pillaging, hunting, and fighting, apparently controlled by no one and certainly respecting neither Church, man, nor, especially, maiden.

For example, *the Anglo-Saxon Chronicle* for the year 1137, in the midst of the century claimed by most authorities to be the golden age of chivalry, vividly describes those barons who, the threat of barbaric invasion removed, now fought the onslaughts of nationalism and centralized government:

Every peaceful man made his castles and held them against the king. They filled them with devils and scoundrels, and they seized those persons that they thought had property and put them in prison and tortured them with unutterable torments; for never were martyrs tortured as they were. They hanged them up by the feet and smoked them with foul smoke; they suspended them by the thumbs or by the head and hung armour on their feet; they put knotted strings about their heads and twisted them so that they went into the brain. They put them into dungeons in which there were adders and snakes and toads and so killed them. . . . However a man tilled, the earth bare no corn; for the land was all foredone by such deeds. And men said openly that Christ and his saints slept.[8]

There is little point in laboring the obvious. The documents of all nations covering the years from the coronation of Charlemagne to the Council of Clermont in 1095 and the establishment of the great crusading orders early in the twelfth century and even beyond are filled with horrific accounts of the outrages of these warrior knights. The day of the battle axe and mace, of the need for slaughter and self-preservation had passed, but its institutions and its customs, its tournaments and petty wars, lived on. And the knight, whether baron or member of the new eleventh-century subsidiary nobility,[9] was too firmly a part of the social and economic system to be removed. If the civilization of Europe was ever to shake off the brutality of the Dark Ages, then the knight, by this time an anachronism, had first to be put to use and then to be softened.

The Crusades put him to use. Although the concept of the Christian soldier is at least as old as Augustine, the Church had never, even though it had long since abandoned its early pacifism, actually advocated or condoned war, but the spread of Islam, itself firmly committed to a doctrine of conversion by the sword, made holy war inevitable in the West. The series of victories won by the Turks over the Byzantine Christian forces culminating in the capture of Jerusalem in 1073, the urgent appeals from the eastern Church to the western, the preaching of Peter the Hermit and other God-fired zealots, the official proclamations of Rome—all these served to awaken in the military and noble castes of Europe an awareness of a cause greater than their own feudal bickerings. No historian believes that in those early days the urge to save the holy places of the East was the primary moving factor of the first Crusades. The simple urges to travel, fight, and acquire still more land probably first motivated more knights than did the arguments of even the most inflamed preachers. Yet as the First Crusade assembled and moved eastward, a change could be seen in the motives of the crusading knights. The desire to fight and win was supplanted, or at least augmented, by the desire to punish the heathen. Personal reputation, the love of glory, was never far from the mind of the crusading knight of any year, but religious devotion, a genuine piety of arms, and the desire for salvation joined the older, more primitive ambition.

It is usual to say that Christian chivalry emerges from

feudal knighthood at this point and, to a large extent, this is exactly what does happen. But the conversion is less spectacular and less complete than it first appears. Even the great crusading orders—the Hospitallers, the Teutonic Knights, the Knights Templars, and the others —with their elaborate semi-religious ceremonials and badges never quite succeeded in reaching the ideal standard set by the Church. The new petty nobility might insist that individually acquired prowess and honor were more important than inherited riches, but it is impossible to avoid atrocities in war, and no fighting man, no matter how idealistic his cause, can avoid completely the brutalities of combat. Thus, contemporaneous accounts of crusading knights at times show the same ferocious disregard for human life, the same love of torture and pillage, as the accounts of earlier warriors.

But the Church and the Crusades had at least provided the knight with a *raison d'être* capable of governing his life both in the field and in the castle. He could remain a soldier, but he might now be also a Christian soldier, employed by the Church in her never-ending war against evil both in the Holy Land and at home. It would be too much, perhaps, to say that the Church realized that in converting knighthood to the service of Christianity she had struck her greatest blow in the great war of Pope and Emperor that dominates the medieval political scene from Constantine to the Renaissance. However, as the Crusades went on, the Crusaders did in fact come more and more to think of themselves as bound to the Church, rather than to any particular secular authority. For the Church had now come to control, certainly in spirit and often in detailed operation, the life of the knight—his education, his training, his investiture with its oaths and rituals, and, in fact, his whole career. Thus, in peace as well as in war, knighthood became an arm of the Church enforcing her political rights and her moral standards throughout the western world.

But the gulf between theory and practice still remained.

It should be understood that even the best crusading knight—and there were many knights who like Tancred of Sicily and Godfrey of Bouillon took very seriously their obligations as soldiers of Christ—still lacked the one element that most characterizes our idealized twentieth-century conception of him. At this period his oaths, largely through the influence of the Church, included the defense of the oppressed, the widowed, and the orphaned. He was enjoined to protect women of noble birth, but he was not as yet the lover, the courtier, the gallant.

We do not know a great deal about the beginnings of courtly love in Europe. Presumably it is a phenomenon of Eastern origin introduced into southern Europe, perhaps by the returning Crusaders, perhaps by the Moors, perhaps by both. Strictly speaking, courtly love is described most accurately as a relationship between the sexes in which the woman is exalted to a position of dominance and the lover becomes a loyal servant who must pass a series of tests to advance from the horrors of the "malady of love" to the ecstatic possession of the beloved. Its characteristic features, according to C. S. Lewis, are humility, courtesy, adultery, and the religion of love.[10] But any such terse description of the relationship of lover and lady, even the codified account of Andreas Capellanus, fails to indicate the real importance of courtly love in western society. For courtly love was more than a particular codification of accepted behavior, the sort of thing Margaret Mead writes about. It was a complete social revolution, the effects of which are still apparent in the culture of western Europe and America.[11]

Man in the classical ages and in the early Middle

Ages had never regarded woman as being in any way his equal. Thus, while he had revered and esteemed his friends and found friendship and honor well worth dying for, he had never regarded love of woman as being of any serious consequence. It is clear, for example, that Achilles sulks in his tent not because of the loss of Briseis—who later reports that only Patroclus treated her decently—but because Agamemnon had violated *aidos*, the proper working relationship of men in a man's world. As C. S. Lewis amply has shown,[12] the *Ars Amatoria*, taken at its face value in the Middle Ages, clearly is satirical in nature; "only a fool," Ovid is saying, "would ever act like this," pointing to what is obviously the love-sick swain of the mid twentieth-century culture, all "starry-eyed and vaguely discontented." Certainly women in the Middle Ages were regarded generally as little better than chattel, fit only for domestic work and child bearing.[13]

Thus, suddenly to insist, as did the Provençal poets, that the true object of man's love and respect and devotion and loyalty and desire was not his companion, or even his lord, but his lord's wife, who because of her social station and marriage (which was, by the way, nearly always a matter of convenience) was unattainable by any normal standards of conduct—to insist on this was to thrust the knight into the midst of a conflict for which his training and disposition left him totally unprepared.

For courtly love plummeted the knight, the fighting machine who had been first an ironclad barbaric bully and then an ironclad Christian bully, into two dilemmas, two sets of incompatible choices which he could not avoid if he were to retain the responsibilities of a knight and the added duties of a lover. For no matter how finely tempered, how delicately sensitive the relationship between lover and lady might be, the courtly lover was forced by the system to be untrue to both his older masters, his lord and his Church.[14] The natural end, the only possible successful end of the lover's suit, was adultery with his lord's wife, and adultery is a sin against both loyalty and religion.[15] The doctrine of courtly love introduced into the practice of chivalry complications and contradictions of such magnitude that no concept of the worth of knighthood, no matter how idealistic, could fail to sense the tragic inconsistency not simply between theory and practice, ideal and real, but within the theory itself.

From the outset, courtly love was condemned by the Church as unalterably opposing the Church's strictures against adultery and the Church's position that in marriage the husband, not the wife, held final sovereignty. However, courtly love, though condemned, flourished, protected and encouraged by the rich and powerful; it moved quickly into northern France and on, through the marriage of Eleanor of Aquitaine to Henry II of England, across the English Channel. If courtly love carried with it a justification of adultery and intrigue, it carried also a code of manners which more than any other single factor transformed the court of Hygelac into the court of Bercilak and Sir Bruce Without Pity into Lancelot. "Behold you," says Aimeric de Pégulhan, one of the troubadours, "the good things which love gives: it makes a vile creature into a distinguished man, a fool into a man of agreeable conversation, a miser into a spendthrift, and it transforms a rascal into a man of honor. By it insane men become sages, the gauche become polished and the haughty are changed into gentle and humble men."[16]

The gallant lover, the new knight, could at least theoretically no longer rely simply upon raw muscle as a means of acquiring fame; he now had to impress his lady with fair words and music and flawless manners and dress. His training now came to emphasize not only the martial and sporting skills—proficiency in arms, in horse-manship, in falconry—but also the courtly arts—music, poetry, dress. The set periods of training—pagedom and squireage—remained, but the virtues of courtly behavior, what later comes to be called *gentilesse*, gradually is seen to dominate the training; humility, courtesy, and the religion of love replace, or at least supplement, the warlike ideals of earlier ages.

The integration of courtly love into the knightly code in the period extending roughly over the twelfth and thirteenth centuries not only makes the knight fit for the hall and the bower as well as for the battlefield, but it also makes him fit for literature. We have, of course, no purely literary records of the early knights. A civilization actually engaged in fighting for its existence has no time for belle-lettres. Only after the uses of peace have come to supplant those of war and the court has replaced the castle is there time to analyze and consider the experiences of the past and to present them, as Aristotle said literature always does, as philosophy, as patterned and meaningful experience, rather than as mere history. But in the process of reviewing the past and of recreating it in the epic, heroic form that experiences of this kind almost invariably take, the mind of the writer, especially the medieval writer more intent on meaning than on surface verisimilitude, on *sens* rather than *matière*, comes to confuse time and place. This is why Shakespeare "fills Ilion, Rome, or any town you like / Of olden time with timeless English-men"[17] and why the eleventh-century author of the *Song of Roland* transforms a minor military action of the year 778, a routine skirmish in which a Basque guerrilla force intent only on spoils attacked and destroyed the rearguard of Charlemagne's forces, into an epic of the worldwide struggle of Cross and Crescent involving heroes more legendary than real and utilizing a "cast of thousands."

In short, thirteenth-century writers of the chivalric, courtly lays and romances, of whatever dramatic date, picture only the knight of their own time, and they almost invariably picture him in an idealized form as the courteous, humane, gentle knight who without blemish or stain rides about dispensing justice and mercy.

I have devoted more space than perhaps is necessary in such a cursory and loosely drawn survey as this to the effects of courtly love upon knighthood because the courtly lover becomes the knight of late medieval literature. I am not prepared to argue whether or not courtly love was a real social phenomenon or merely a literary convention; I suspect that it could never have influenced literature as it did without having some existence in fact. But real or literary, the courtly lover-knight is the only knight who appears as the hero of the courtly romances[18] of the period because he is the only knight to bear within himself and in his way of life the complex and ambivalent raw materials from which great literature can be made. It is courtly love also which supplies the knight not only with a character, a set of values, and a potential conflict capable of literary treatment, but with an occupation— knight errantry—out of which plot and action may be constructed. Certainly the real knight, at any period preceding the eleventh century, had little, if any, time to go off a-questing. He had at first to defend his castle and later his religion, and for both these causes he fought in a group. Only the courtly lover in time of peace had time to go out alone wandering about the countryside, and courtly love alone gives him a motive for wandering—the fulfillment of the vows made to his lady.

There are a number of discernible stages in the progress of the lover from first sight of his lady to final possession of her, though, of course, no single lover need experience all of them. His falling in love is immediate and complete. In the fanciful, though nevertheless accurate, psychology of the Middle Ages the lover is shot in the eye by the God of Love, the arrow descending immediately to the heart. The lover approaches the lady directly, but generally he presses his suit too forcefully and is repulsed. He falls into despair, ravaged by the terrors of the malady of love—sleeplessness, loss of appetite, a kind of self-pitying melancholy, and, most importantly, a temporary and bewildering loss of hope. At this point he throws himself, often by means of a go-between, upon the mercy of the lady, and she, through pity, agrees to accept him as her servant, though not as yet as her lover.

Our interest lies at this point in the process. For precisely here, at the stage when the knight is still a suitor and his possession of the beloved is still far from accomplished, he becomes in the romances, if not perhaps in life, a knight errant, a young chevalier on the quest of *aventure*. He seeks adventure for only one reason: "to stonden in his lady grace." So he roams the wide world in search of ogres, giants, dragons, and Black Knights of Black Lands to demonstrate, by deeds as well as by poems and songs, that he is essentially worthy of the favors of his beloved.

The best introduction to the questing knight is the romances of Chrétien de Troyes who is both the virtual originator of the genre and its greatest glory. However, the essential qualities of Chrétien's knights—Erec, Yvain, Cliges, Lancelot, Perceval—become clear only when set in some context, literary as well as historical. This context can be supplied by a brief examination of the literary knight as he exists immediately prior to the period of Chrétien. Roland of the *Chanson de Roland* is one of the literary and, by extension, historical forerunners of Chrétien's knights. The poem itself is a *chanson de geste*, and, as the term suggests, the *Chanson de Roland* is concerned primarily with deeds. The deeds of these warriors are magnified in retrospect by poets who already see about them a decline in *virtus* from these "olden times" of heroic valor and sacrifice, but who have not yet perceived the infinitely greater literary possibilities in the new chivalry. For certainly Roland in the poem is of an older breed of hero. Like Lancelot, he is brave, aggressive, proud, and a thorough believer in the social and military system of which he is a part. Like Lancelot, he is a Christian; he fights both for his personal glory and for his God. But unlike Lancelot, Roland is neither lover nor courtier. True, he is presumably in love, and Aude, his fiancé and Oliver's sister, died upon hearing the news of the battle of Roncevaux. But he is most emphatically not a lover; except for a single reference in passing, Aude's name never crosses his lips, and it is clear that, however faithful and devoted Aude may be, Roland fights only for his own glory and that of his religion and that his mind never touches upon her image, not even in death. Roland is, in his standards and values, a knight of an older time, idealized perhaps and certainly softened by a late author, but clearly still a portrait from the past.

Although less than a hundred years separate the writing of the *Chanson de Roland* and *Yvain*, they stand centuries apart in the progress of chivalry. The author of the *Chanson de Roland*, writing late in the eleventh century, is depicting a northern knight of the time of the First Crusade, stylized, but magnificently courageous, strong, and proud. He stands for the world of militaristic chivalry; his values are pride and confidence in his own prowess and devotion to the knightly principles of personal honor (not, please note, the honor of chivalry; otherwise, Roland would have blown the horn to assure a national triumph for the French), loyalty to one's companions, and the truth of the Christian doctrine and cause. These values are, of course, assumed; they are never debated, as are the courtly values of the troubadours, or even questioned. Roland has no conflict of values or ideas, no internal struggle of any kind, and it would be supremely out of character for him to be faced with any essential choice of values. True, he must decide on first entering the battle whether or not to summon Charlemagne, but, in spite of Oliver's protests, he decides, by a simple application of the concept of personal honor to the immediate situation, to refrain from blowing the horn. And we, the audience, are expected, at least in the poet's view, to approve that choice. Oliver cannot resist an "I told you so" at the last, but everyone knows that while Oliver is wise, Roland is proud, and that Roland, not Oliver, is the hero of the poem.

The world in which Roland lives and fights is thus envisioned by the poet as a very simple world, rigidly, and comfortingly, described by the laws of the Church and Emperor. Once the values of such a world are accepted and its standards met, the early knight may go his way in absolute confidence of the rightness of his own conduct. There are no ambiguities of life and death to plague him, no unresolved relationships, either in heaven or earth, to give him a moment's uneasiness. Archbishop Turpin assures the French host that since he has blest and absolved them before battle and since they will die with Saracen blood on their swords, they are assured of martyrdom and will sit on high in Paradise. And in a line which epitomizes perfectly the blend of piety and ferocity that characterizes the Crusader, Turpin bids them "to strike for their penance."[19]

This fundamental rigidity of code and narrowness of outlook is peculiar to the French *chansons de geste* and seems more than any other feature to set them apart from other epic and heroic literature. The French knight of the *chansons de geste*, even the Lord Roland himself, may impress us with his unfailing heroism, his dauntless courage, his matchless prowess; but his life and even his death are in the end matters of small concern, because in the end his life and death do not touch ours and his world is not our world. Roland's world is too simple, his choices too prescribed, his death, paradoxically, too easy. Hector, Gunnar, Hagan, and Lancelot are real to us, overpoweringly so at times, by virtue of their weaknesses and the complexities of the problems they face. Roland dies assured of martyrdom and glory; his death is for him, as for his companions, a triumph of the knightly code and the Christian dogma. But for the others, for Achilles and Hector faced with an eternity spent wandering among the dim, unhappy, restless shades to whom, we remember, Patroclus returned "gibbering," for Njal and Gunnar looking forward only to a perpetual war of good and evil in which they eventually will be defeated, for these and for the other heroes of epic literature, life is better than death and their final victories over the fates which propel them on to destruction are not granted them simply by their membership in the Church or even by their loyalty to a code, but by virtue of their personal, hard won decisions to stand and fight. Hector stops at the gate of Troy and Achilles stays on the battlefield both knowing that they are deliberately choosing death rather than shame and dishonor, and knowing also that their deaths will in the long run profit no one. And Gunnar dies a useless death rather than force from Hallgerd, his spiteful, worthless wife, a few strands of her hair to restring his bow. Balin, Malory's ill-fated knight with two swords, says on hearing far off a hunting horn, "That blast is blowen for me, for I am the pryse, and yet am I not dede."[20] And so he rides knowingly into death.

Although Roland and the heroes of these early poems

may be heroic, they are neither tragic nor even sympathetically human. This is a point essential to any clear understanding of what happens less than one hundred years later to the figure of the knight. It is a commonplace of literary judgment to regard the *Chanson de Roland* as somehow being a more "realistic" work, defined in the most obvious terms of surface verisimilitude,[21] than the courtly romances of Chrétien and his followers. Yet a closer reading reveals, I think, the reverse. The *Chanson de Roland* is a myth of chivalric battle, fought by peerless Christians against heathen devils—"Pagans are wrong and Christians are right"[22]—yet the two groups are indistinguishable, even in that area where they should differ profoundly, the conduct of battle. The French are commanded by a king some 200 years old who is personally attended by angels and at whose request the sun stands still. The odds against which Roland and Oliver fight—several hundred thousand against twenty thousand at the outset, later forty thousand against three lone French warriors—are hyperbolic numbers and could never have been meant by the poet as anything other than figures symbolic of the enormousness of Roland's task.

Thus the *Chanson de Roland* is not realistic even on the surface level of action, and those who deem it more realistic than the romances that follow it do so, I expect, only because it does not contain either dragons or magicians. On the psychological level also, that of character and motive and conflict, the poem never for a moment rings true. Thus although, as we shall see, the romances of Chrétien are filled with the most monumental excesses of conduct and utilize magicians and even dragons, they do not seek to escape the problems of the present by elevating and idealizing the events of the past. The conflicts, the tortuous dilemmas of courtly love and chivalric loyalty, of the choice between Venus and Christ, true and false felicity, infiltrate even the most serene of the romances and so begin to divide the castle against itself.

But before this can happen, the knight must leave the ranks of battle at Roncevaux and ride off alone into the fields and forests of Logres.

THE USES OF LOVE

CHRÉTIEN'S KNIGHTS

I T HAPPENED seven years ago that, lonely as a countryman,
I was making my way in search of adventures, fully armed
as a knight should be, when I came upon a road leading
off to the right into a thick forest. The road there was very
bad, full of briars and thorns. In spite of the trouble and
inconvenience, I followed the road and path. Almost the
entire day I went thus riding until I emerged from the forest
of Broceliande. Out from the forest I passed into the open
country where I saw a wooden tower at the distance of half
a Welsh league: it may have been so far, but it was not any
more. Proceeding faster than a walk, I drew near and saw
the palisade and moat all round it, deep and wide, and
standing upon the bridge, with a moulted falcon upon his
wrist, I saw the master of the castle.[1]

It is another world, is it not? There is nothing here
of the blood-soaked forest at Roncevaux, nothing of the
stout feudal brotherhood of arms, of men standing and
fighting for the Cross against insuperable hordes of
pagans. The knight (his name here is Calogrenant) is
now a wanderer searching for *aventure* and in his quest

encountering marvels and trials beyond the imagination of Roland or Godfrey of Bouillon. He is also an almost purely literary figure.

For we have moved now from epic to romance, from the heroic age to the age of chivalry, and such a journey entails not only a shift in the scheme of action through which the knight moves, but a shift also in the set of values for which he stands. As W. P. Ker says, one has only to see for a moment in his mind's eye the "victory of the Norman knights over the English axemen"[2] at Hastings to perceive the two images within a single frame, the stolid Saxon nobility fighting on foot in closed ranks, maneuvering and striking by the tactical principles of Brunanburgh and Maldon, while the French, mounted, mobile, gallant, launch cavalry attack upon cavalry attack until a storm of French arrows fired high into the air destroys the inner ranks of the Saxon force and the mounted French knights, the new chivalry, disperse forever the heroic age in England.

The progress from the simple agrarian social structure and court life of the heroic age to the more complex socio-economic structure of late feudalism was inevitable. As western Europe recovered its poise and security after the Dark Ages, it began to adopt new values and life patterns. As we have seen, the court replaced the castle, the courtly knight the brutal warrior, and the tangled thread of feudal relationships the simple loyalties of the *comites*.[3] The new literature reflects, as does all literature, these changes. Epic literature is a stately, solemn celebration of national life in the heroic age. Its heroes are simple men, versed in the activities of common life— hunting, law, farming and cooking; they are leaders not through class status or wealth or even birth, but through the excellencies of heart and mind and hands. Their motives are linked with the practical necessities of life, and they share a tragic view of existence, through which they and the reader are constantly made aware of the instability of earthly things and the inevitability of man's fate.

But the epic hero can live only in a heroic age.[4] The new feudalism with its leisure and highly stratified class structure demanded a new hero, a man attuned to the niceties of conduct and indoctrinated in the values of courtly life. The chivalric romance is thus elegant rather than plain, fluent rather than stately, sentimental rather than tragic. The great solid magnificence of the epic form is replaced by a swiftly moving plot in which variety of incident and strangeness of adventure dominate the action. The simple motives of the epic hero—the protection of his land, home, and honor—yield to those of the knightly adventurer, whose reasons for action are often lost in mazes of psychological probing.

The greatest difference between epic and romance, however, may be observed in that aspect in which the two superficially most resemble one another. Most epics, like most romances, revolve about a journey, a quest. Odysseus is searching for a home and Aeneas a homeland, and Erec, Yvain, and Perceval are pursuing various ideals, captured ladies, menacing castles, or hidden relics. In both epic and romance the hero must undergo hardships in attaining his object, and he is frequently led astray through chance or defeat or indolence from the straight road leading to his destination.

But certain differences in the nature of the two quests, heroic and romantic, are apparent. The epic hero is propelled by destiny, *fato profugus*, and his whole journey bears witness to the fact that the desires and purposes of the gods must be achieved on earth through the efforts of men, which all too often flag and are distracted. Upon the epic hero lies always the shadow of a god, Athena or

Venus or simply *Wyrd*, who can be counted on to assist, command, or admonish at the proper time and so secure the demands of history, to reestablish tranquility in Ithaca, to found Rome, or to cleanse Heorot.

And, perhaps more important, the fulfillment of the gods' desire, the attainment of the hero's purpose, is the end toward which the epic moves. When Aeneas reaches the site of Rome the story is over. Even though it frequently begins *in medias res*, the epic generally involves a relatively simple straight line narrative leading by events arranged in mounting sequence from epic question to epic conclusion, from challenge to fulfillment. The epic hero, willy-nilly, plays out in no uncertain terms the great role in history fate has chosen for him.

The quest of the early knight errant is different in structure and emphasis, if not quite in kind. The epic is indigenous both to a nation and a religion; the romance, on the other hand, is exotic, the product of a particular sophisticated social group, rather than of a whole culture. The adventures of the knight errant thus follow a more devious path, less predetermined and directed. First, unlike the epic hero, he is unattended by gods and unaided by epic machinery, even in those romances which have as heroes the great figures of the classical world. He is no founder of nations; he has no historical role to play out. If the knight errant has a destiny arranged for him by Heaven, he is never aware of it, and the author and reader seem unaware of it also. The reader presumes, of course, that Yvain will eventually find his way back to the fountain and that Erec and Enide will work out their difficulties, but he is not persuaded that the hero triumphs by the express will of the gods or is aided by heavenly forces.

This is not to say that the romance hero does not receive divine assistance; Gawain discovers Bercilak's castle immediately upon praying for some harbor where he may hear Mass, and Lancelot's healing of Sir Urry is a direct answer to prayer, but actions such as these are few and widely separated. The romantic knight is mostly unguided and roams an apparently purposeless universe in search of an object which usually seems increasingly vague even to him.

But I use the terms "apparently" and "seems" deliberately. For in spite of the superficial aimlessness of the medieval romance, there does seem to be present at least in the first romances, those of Chrétien de Troyes, a pattern of action, evidence of some direction in the twisted route which the literary knight follows.

In an important article Professor William S. Woods demonstrated that four of Chrétien's romances—*Guillaume d'Angleterre, Erec et Enide,* the *Chevalier au Lion,* and the *Conte del Graal*—could be reduced to a general plot formula:

A hero achieves the realization of his worldly ambitions and desires in an introductory passage. He is then made aware of some error or fault or of some less obvious reason which forces him to abandon his lofty pinnacle of happiness. This point in the plot can be likened to the initial impulse of a drama for it serves to motivate the main body of the poem which is a series of adventures concerned with the hero's efforts to recover his former status, presumably through his becoming more deserving of it by the correction of his error or by the expiation of his fault.[5]

Although Professor Woods is content simply with demonstrating the existence of this pattern of action in Chrétien and with delineating the problems of motivation and consistency of character it raises, he points out that such a pattern in Chrétien's major works suggests that actions that seem illogical and ill-contrived on the level of *matière* may on the level of *sens* be logical and significant.

Like Woods, I think that Chrétien is in these romances dealing with an ordered pattern of action which appears not only in the plot formula, but in the idea of knighthood and the knightly quest that underlies that plot. Perhaps we have been led astray in examining Chrétien's plots by undue attention to two considerations: first, by our inclination to attribute to Chrétien all the ambiguity of motive and plot that mars the genre after Chrétien's own time, and, second, by our insistence on locating only one kind of plot pattern in Chrétien, the direct movement from problem to solution that descends from the epic into the modern novel.

While Chrétien's plots do of course fit this pattern in the broad general sense in which all literature can be said to deal with conflict and resolution, upon closer inspection they do not conform to the exact requirements of the type. They demonstrate, as Professor Woods points out, a disjointed double structure unlike the single movement of the ordinary tale. *Erec et Enide, Lancelot,* and *Yvain* do not move in one uninterrupted line; the central period of conflict of each is preceded by a fully developed action in which their heroes settle major issues of public and private life and come to a firm and, one would think, lasting arrangement with the world. The first fourth of *Erec et Enide* deals with a "preliminary" action in which Erec courts and wins the beautiful Enide, and the problem that underlies the main action of *Yvain* is not introduced until the poem has run well over one third of its length. These initial actions, however, cannot be regarded as mere preludes to the events that follow them; they are in fact major parts of the poems' plots. We have before us, quite obviously, a plot structure different from that with which we generally are called upon to deal, a pattern of action which finds its roots and springs in a set of responses to life and in a narrative tradition older than the journeys of Odysseus, in a pattern of quest and attainment of which the traditional epic structure is a late variant.

The myth of the hero's quest is so ancient and widespread as both to obviate and defy definition. As Joseph Campbell states,[6] it is the monomyth, the center of reality as perceived by creative man in all ages and nations and under a number of forms of expression—ritual, myth, scripture, dream, even history. The hero myth recounts man's perpetual, instinctive attempt to withdraw, to journey from the outer to the inner world to find there the never-failing springs of new life and to return to his old existence bringing new energy and insight. Heinrich Zimmer[7] sees this principle as the operative factor in all successful psychoanalysis, the individual's search for his true identity in the dark, largely forgotten mazes of past experience. Arnold Toynbee sees it as the key to understanding the rise and fall of nations and cultures. Increasing numbers of literary critics use the pattern of the hero's quest to come to grip with literature.

It is possible that a great many of the historians, literary critics, and psychologists who are using so dramatically the questing myth as a panacea for all their ills are in fact overusing the method. But there is little doubt that the myth pattern does embody, in a simple and usable form, a principle of reality so vast as to have implications for nearly every area of life. Joseph Campbell after examining hundreds of versions of the quest myth sums up the basic pattern by means of a diagram and an extended formula:

The mythological hero, setting forth from his commonday hut or castle, is lured, carried away, or else voluntarily proceeds, to the threshold of adventure. There he encounters a shadow presence that guards the passage. The hero may defeat or conciliate this power and go alive into the kingdom of the dark (brother-battle, dragon-battle; offering, charm), or be slain by the opponent and descend in death. . . . Beyond the threshold, then, the hero journeys through a world of unfamiliar yet strangely intimate forces, some of which severely threaten him (tests), some of which give magical aid (helpers). When he arrives at the nadir of the mytho-logical round, he undergoes a supreme ordeal and gains his reward. The triumph may be represented as the hero's sexual union with the goddess-mother of the world . . . , his recogni-tion by the father-creator . . . , his own divination . . . , or again—if the powers have remained unfriendly to him—his theft of the boon he came to gain. . . . The final work is that of the return. If the powers have blessed the hero, he now sets forth under their protection . . . ; if not, he flees and is pursued. . . . The boon that he brings restores the world (elixir).[8]

In the more familiar terms of Arnold Toynbee, the hero caught in the static, sterile perfection of Yin must some-how break out into the world outside his shell:

In every case the story opens with a perfect state of Yin. Faust is perfect in knowledge; Job is perfect in goodness and prosperity; Adam and Eve are perfect in innocence and ease; the Virgins—Gretchen, Danae, and the rest—are perfect in purity and beauty. In the astronomer's universe the Sun, a perfect orb, travels on its course intact and whole. When Yin is thus complete, it is ready to pass over into Yang. But what is to make it pass? A change in a state which, by definition, is perfect after its kind can only be started by an impulse or motive which comes from outside. If we think of the state as one of physical equilibrium, we must bring in another star. If we think of it as one of psychic beatitude or *nirvana*, we must bring another actor to the stage: a critic to set the mind thinking again by suggesting doubts; an adversary to set the heart feeling again by instilling distress or discontent or fear or antipathy.[9]

The summaries of the hero's quest by Campbell and Toynbee closely parallel Professor Woods' summary of Chrétien's romances. By this I do not mean to imply that Chrétien was involved with or interested in myth, at least as myth is conceived of by Campbell and Toynbee, but I do mean to suggest Chrétien's romances reflect to a great extent and in a remarkably "pure," though highly individualized, form the essential movements of the mythic hero.

Actually, the epics adhere more closely in at least one respect to the patterns of the myth than do the romances; they manifest clearly in the journeys of their heroes, as Chrétien's knights do not, the sense of destiny, the *fato profugus* which the myth itself sometimes assumes. But despite this loss, attributable almost certainly to the medieval audience's love of digression, the basic pattern of the hero's journey still shapes both *sens* and *matière* in Chrétien, and an understanding of that pattern is vital to our understanding of his poems.

One particular manifestation of the hero myth is the *rites de passage*, the initiatory rites of primitive people, marking the passage of the initiate from youth to maturity. Although such rites obviously mark the physical changes of puberty, they celebrate changes in the initiate's psychological and spiritual nature as well. Thus the rites of passage, like most primitive rituals concerned with the great events of life, tend to symbolize their own processes and meaning, and reflect, as Eliade has demonstrated, the primitive's attempt to find the reality and meaning of temporal existence by recreating and reenacting outside of time and space the divine models of behavior laid down by the gods. Such rituals, in fact, "acquire the meaning attributed to them, and materialize that meaning, only because they deliberately repeat such and such acts posited *ab origine* by gods, heroes, or ancestors."[10] It is not surprising, therefore, that in most of these initiatory rites, the youth is first of all thrust apart for a time from the tribe and his severance accompanied by drastic and severe acts, normally including circumcision, which make clear the width of the gulf he is crossing. Then presented to him in isolation are ritual actions that introduce to him the duties and secrets of his new life. Most important, he learns these matters in isolation, often in darkness, completely cut off from his family and from any reminders of his former life. At length he emerges from this extended retirement a new man, ready to take his place as a fully indoctrinated citizen of the tribe, and usually ready to establish a new place of residence in the village.

Obviously, the major symbols of such rites symbolize a death to the static world of childhood and a rebirth into a dynamic adult world. The ritual marks for initiate and tribe the "road leading to the center" of existence, "arduous, fraught with perils, because it is, in fact, a rite of the passage from the profane to the sacred, from the ephemeral and illusory to reality and eternity, from death to life, from man to the divinity."[11] The comfortable relationship of mother and father and child and the safe, friendly protected world of toys and games—and how like the medieval court it all is—is dramatically rejected as unfit for the adult. Thus by means of complex symbolic actions, the initiate understands that he has died forever to his former life and has been reborn to a life incomparably richer.

While such rituals of withdrawal and return are simply one manifestation of the more inclusive hero myth, they nevertheless indicate more clearly than can the larger, more generalized pattern designated by Campbell the redemptive, regenerative nature of the myth. For the individual hero, whether savage or knight, the quest is a death to his old life, however comfortable and secure that life may have been, because it is not capable of developing his latent creative powers; and it is the discovery, through trial and conflict, of principles and ideas capable of carrying him into modes of action impossible in his former life.

I think that the romances of Chrétien deal precisely, though in general terms and in symbols and patterns unknown perhaps even to him, with this *rite de passage*, this death and rebirth, this journey of the hero into the unknown and back. *Erec et Enide* provides a beginning.

The poem begins with the stable social situation typical of all romances: "One Easter Day in the Springtime, King Arthur held court in his town of Cardigan" (1). Arthur, following a custom, institutes a hunt for the White Stag, the winner of which may kiss the fairest maiden of the court. The queen, accompanied by the unarmed Erec, son of King Loc, witnesses an injury to one of her maidens by a dwarf, the servant of an evil-tempered knight. Erec, in attempting to find an explanation for the dwarf's actions, is whipped and, leaving the queen, follows the knight and dwarf through the forest into a large town.

To this point the pattern seems obvious. Erec has met with the strange messenger of the myths and has received a call to adventure. Moreover, he has responded to this call in no uncertain terms by following the dwarf across the forest barrier and through the threshold gate into the land of trials, the gaily-bedecked town. Here Erec is received by a vavasour who explains there is to be a game the next day in which worthy knights may claim a hawk in the name of their ladies and defend the hawk from challenges. Erec defends the hawk in the name of

Enide, the daughter of the vavasour, against Yder, the insolent knight whose dwarf had whipped Erec. Inspired by the sight of Enide, Erec wins. Erec then restores the fortunes of the vavasour and leads Enide back to Arthur's court where she is judged the most beautiful of all the maidens and awarded by Arthur the kiss of the White Stag.

At this point, says Chrétien, the first part of his story ends. To all appearances it has been a most successful story: Erec has met the challenge; he has won his lady love and has returned from the strange unknown land bearing the symbols of his triumph—hawk and bride. In his moment of victory he is said to be second only to Gawain in Arthur's esteem.

But from another point of view, Erec's adventure has not been a success, but only a prelude to failure:

When the hero-quest has been accomplished, through pene-tration to the source, or through the grace of some male or female, human or animal, personification, the adventurer must still return with his life-transmuting trophy. The full round, the norm of the monomyth, requires that the hero shall now begin the labor of bringing the runes of wisdom, the Golden Fleece, or his sleeping princess, back into the kingdom of humanity, where the boon may redound to the renewing of the community, the nation, the planet, or the ten thousand worlds.[12]

And even more succinctly:

The withdrawal makes it possible for the personality to realize powers within himself which might have remained dormant if he had not been released for the time being from his social toils and trammels. . . . But a transfiguration in solitude can have no purpose, and perhaps even no meaning, except as a prelude to the return of the transfigured personality into

the social milieu out of which he had originally come: a
native environment from which the human social animal
cannot permanently estrange himself without repudiating his
humanity and becoming, in Aristotle's phrase, 'either a beast
or a god.' The return is the essence of the whole movement
as well as its final cause.[13]

The terms of the myth here shed light upon Erec's
predicament at this point, the point at which Woods
finds all of Chrétien's romances lacking in coherence and
motivation. What has happened is that far from beginning a new story or even a second part of the old one,
we have reached the crisis for which Chrétien has been
preparing us all along. Note how quickly the poet has
maneuvered us through the first sections of the tale—the
call to adventure, the challenge, the crossing of the
threshold, the great battle for the lady—incidents which
normally occupy longest the ordinary romancer. Yet, as
Joseph Campbell says, "the changes rung on the simple
scale of the monomyth defy description," and "many tales
isolate and greatly enlarge upon one or two of the typical
elements of the full cycle. . . ."[14] Chrétien's point of concentration in *Erec et Enide* and the other romances is the
return of the victorious hero from the "other world"
of adventure and enchantment, and his theme the difficulty of that return.

Thus Erec's marriage is not the conclusion of his
adventure but the beginning of its central conflict. In
retiring to his father's estate with his wife and accepting
as final the conditions of his retirement—the festival
welcome, the blessing of the Church, the gifts, the luxury,
the leisure—Erec denies the necessity of using whatever
gift he as hero had earned in the city beyond the forest;
he has, in fact, never returned from that other land.
Thus, "Erec loved her [Enide] with such a tender love

that he cared no more for arms, nor did he go to tournaments, nor have any desire to joust; but he spent his time in cherishing his wife." Soon "all the knights said it was a great pity and misfortune that such a valiant man as he was wont to be should no longer wish to bear arms. He was blamed so much on all sides by the knights and squires that murmurs reached Enide's ears how that her lord had turned craven about arms and deeds of chivalry, and that his manner of life was greatly changed" (32).

The reasons for such a failure to return to reality and duty, both in the myth and in the romance, are obviously a part of the human condition; they are more easily understood than is the failure to accept the challenge. After the battle is won and the boon secured, the return becomes to all appearances a superfluity: "Why re-enter such a world? Why attempt to make plausible, or even interesting, to men and women consumed with passion, the experience of transcendental bliss? . . . The easy thing is to commit the whole community to the devil and retire again into the heavenly rock-dwelling, close the door, and make it fast."[15] This ennui and its cause, the hero's lack of self-knowledge, are the real reasons for Erec's inaction. He is quite willing that the old life go on about him; he will even support it with money and good wishes. But he will not participate in it, nor will he redeem it with his gift, the boon from another world, which he now selfishly and ignorantly employs only for his own enjoyment.

What I have been calling the "boon," the "gift," here needs defining, lest I seem to have replaced the real Enide with a generalized, mythical panacea. According to the terms of the myth, the gift must be a life-transmuting power, an elixir, a grace capable of both energizing and giving meaning to the static equilibrium of the Yin existence. Erec's failure is in refusing to recognize the effect of Enide and her love upon his knighthood. It is essentially the failure to use for any good purpose the prowess or the inspiration to the right use of prowess given to him by Enide. He had at the time of his battle with Yder been given just such a gift by "she of the gentle and open heart"(15) without his realizing it. For at the time of that battle, during a rest interval, while Erec "sat and looked on [Enide], great strength was recruited within him. Her love and beauty inspired him with great boldness" (12). By yielding after his marriage to Luxuria and Uxoria, Erec refuses the responsibility of returning with his life-giving gift to the land of the living, his own world of chivalry, and of using love as a means of redeeming that chivalry.

The great theme of the *Erec et Enide*, the *sens* at which the *matière* aims, is the redemption of chivalry through love, and it is Erec's task at this point in the romance to use the love and power of Enide for something other than personal gratification. But he has rejected the active society of Arthur's court in favor of the isolation of his own castle, and so there he stays entangled in the web of his own withdrawal. He cannot remain inactive forever, and it is significant that Enide in reporting to him the rumors of his defection almost unwittingly is the instrument of his awakening. It is important also to note that Erec immediately accepts as accurate her report of the situation and takes full responsibility for it. It is as though he had known all along that his actions were unbecoming and needed only slight prodding from Enide to admit his guilt. Nor does he hesitate for a moment in accepting this second call to adventure. The solution here is obvious, though Erec does not at this point understand it: he must continue the journey which his excursion into Luxuria interrupted. And Enide, despite her tears, must as before accompany him, even though neither she nor Erec as yet can appreciate fully her importance to him.

Professor Woods objects very strongly to Erec's actions at this point, declaring them essentially unmotivated and all the "subsequent actions . . . almost inexplicable."[16] However, it is almost painfully clear that Chrétien intends us to see that Erec is acting here simply from instinct and is totally ignorant of the forces impelling him to leave the security of his father's house and brave the terrors of the road. His actions are puzzling, but puzzling most of all to himself.[17] He treats Enide roughly, almost with contempt, because he resents her having awakened him from idleness, yet he is careful to make arrangements for her security should he be killed. He orders her to ride before him and to refrain from speaking to him, yet he adds that she may proceed "with confidence"(36). He refuses his father's offer of knights and money, saying that he cannot act in any other way than he does.

His actions on the journey follow the same pattern or, rather, the same ostensible lack of pattern. In the first three of the eight ensuing adventures, Enide is rebuked sharply by Erec for having warned him of the approach of his attackers, though it is clear that she has on all three occasions saved his life. The reader is again aware that Erec is acting totally without judgment, and it is certain that again Erec's irrationality is Chrétien's chief point. Erec seems to move almost in a dream, unconscious of the dangers that surround him, lacking any real sense of purpose. He is obviously a man without direction, hurt and confused, and like most men, and children, in such a situation, willing to blame not himself, but, ironically, the instrument of his salvation. Thus Erec irrationally thinks himself to be testing Enide's love and, like a child, rebukes her for a trifling fault, her failure to keep silence, when her speaking has saved his life.

The fourth adventure marks a change in the pattern. As before, Enide must warn Erec of the approach of an enemy, but though he again threatens her, he "has no desire to do her harm, for he realizes and knows full well that she loves him above all else, and he loves her, too, to the utmost"(49). This statement, heralding a return to health and sanity in Erec, marks the beginning of a change in his conduct. From this point on, he no longer distrusts Enide, and the relations between the two of them improve steadily.

But Chrétien indicates clearly that Erec has not yet crossed the return threshold. True, he has begun to perceive the essential worth of his wife, and he has regained something of his old prowess and self-confidence, but he is not yet ready to rejoin the society of men. The fifth of his eight adventures tempts him to repeat his first mistake, to return prematurely to his proper sphere, his lesson not yet learned. Bruised and bleeding, Erec is accosted by Kay and later by Gawain, both of whom insist that he lodge with Arthur's court, which is nearby. Erec refuses both knights, saying that he must hurry on his journey. Finally tricked into accepting Arthur's hospitality and care, he refuses to stay more than a single night, because, as he says three times, he must continue his journey whatever the price. And as before, he refuses any escort.

This demonstrates, I think, that the irritable purposelessness of Erec's departure from home and his irrational conduct in the first four adventures have now begun to yield to a steady purposiveness in action. For he now values Enide as something more than a pretty toy, and he recognizes some purpose in his wandering. The journey has become a necessity, and though physically exhausted, he stoutly rejects the temptation of Arthur's hospitality.

The ensuing adventures demonstrate actively both Erec's resolution and a new state of affairs between the lovers. For the first time, Erec becomes aware of adventure's approach before Enide does, and, ordering Enide to remain behind, he restores to a damsel a knight tortured by two giants. He then returns as quickly as he can to Enide, for whose safety he is greatly concerned. Not only are the relations of the lovers here for the first time on a normal basis, but for the first time also Erec succeeds in accomplishing an adventure *on behalf of someone other than himself*. He has only now in short regained the status and degree of chivalry he had attained immediately prior to his marriage.

The last two adventures complete the pattern by demonstrating the heights to which chivalric action, *properly motivated by love*, may attain. The seventh adventure, symbolically the most remarkable of all, is essentially Enide's. The battle with the giants and his frantic rush to rejoin Enide cause Erec's wounds to open, and he falls into a faint. Enide takes him to be dead and bitterly reproaches herself for his death. At this point, Count Oringle of Limors comes along, has Erec transported to Limors, and in a sudden burst of passion, marries Enide despite her protests. Then when Enide refuses even to eat and drink at his table, Oringle strikes her twice. The ensuing commotion in the court wakes Erec who, amidst cries of "Flee, flee, here comes the corpse!", rescues Enide and kills Count Oringle. At the end of this adventure Erec's trust in Enide is complete.

The point is, I think, that this strange adventure provides Enide with a temptation which she unhesitatingly rejects. It also provides Erec with proof that not only is his lady faithful, but that she is also, more importantly, essential to his welfare; without her aid he would have died following his encounter with the giants.

And it is Enide also who intervenes immediately following the Count Oringle adventure to save Erec from sure death at the hands of Guivret, who does not recognize his friend. Moreover, this episode provides the reader with a symbolic enactment of Erec's rebirth in the dramatic "Flee, flee, here comes the corpse!" (66). Here for the first time too, Erec obviously feels his journey to be over, or at least almost over, and he remains for some time in the castle of Guivret's sisters to allow his wounds to heal. Here too, Erec and Enide, her beauty now restored after the hardships of the journey, resume normal marital relations. Most important, however, Erec declares his intention of riding as quickly as he can to Arthur's court, obviously now feeling himself worthy to join that society, as he certainly did not feel at the time of the fifth adventure.

The concluding adventure, that of the "Joy of the Court," is in many ways an extrusion; the pattern of the tale, as Chrétien realizes, is complete without it. Yet it provides a kind of apotheosis, the archetypal adventure of the perfect knight. The great difficulties and dangers of the adventure are mysteriously hinted at by King Evrain, and it is interesting to observe Erec's almost limitless self-confidence; "the greater the wonder and the more perilous the adventure, the more he covets it and yearns for it . . ." (73). And even though in his recovered glory, Erec can now undertake combat without Enide, she nevertheless goes with him to the point of battle and is the first to welcome him back. Also, as Jean Frappier states, "the successful hero [has] a more than mortal stature, a superiority even to the supernatural"[18] and so becomes in the terms of Zimmer and Campbell the true hero, ruler of both worlds.

The adventure of the "Joy of the Court" is itself instructive in that it deals with the debilitating effects of love, just as the *Erec et Enide* as a whole deals with its ennobling, vitalizing aspects. Mabonagrain yields to his sweetheart's demand that he never leave her side until forced to by defeat in arms. The fault apparently is the lady's; by this device she had hoped to imprison her knight forever. Yet her own version of the story seems to attach equal blame to Mabonagrain who, she says, swore always to be her lover and could not wait to bring her to the enchanted garden in which they live, a sterile hothouse analogous to Erec's own castle from which he had to flee in order to escape the Luxuria into which he, like Mabonagrain, had fallen.

There is little need to dwell on the protracted conclusion of *Erec et Enide*. It is in essence a description of Erec's new status, first as a knight of Arthur's court and then, through the ritual of coronation, as a king in his own right, and its purpose is to demonstrate beyond any doubt the great honor that has come to the new Erec, the Erec who has successfully braved the trials and dangers of the return journey.

Thus, it seems clear that the subject of *Erec et Enide* is chivalry itself, and the theme of the poem is the relationship of love to valor within the chivalric frame. *The Knight of the Lion* or *Yvain* deals with the same subject and theme, though from a different point of view.

A number of commentators have pointed out that the plot structure of *Yvain* is much like that of *Erec et Enide*. "In the first part of the story," says Julian Harris, "the plot goes from one incident to the next with something approaching breath-taking swiftness, but in the second, it seems to become bogged down in a series of more or less unrelated episodes which are so involved and so interwoven with each other that some readers have difficulty even in following the story."[19] And it seems clear also that Chrétien's narrative in those first adventures again follows the quest myth, even more closely than the opening of *Erec et Enide*. Yvain, starting out from Arthur's court to test Calogrenant's story of a marvelous fountain and the knight who defends it, follows the dark road through the forest, is directed by a kindly vavasour and his beautiful daughter and by an ugly rustic lout, the guardians of the threshold, and successfully passes the threshold of the enchanted other world by defeating the knight of the fountain. Here, through the agency of a young lady-in-waiting, Lunette, he marries the widow of the dead knight and as lord of both worlds is able to entertain lavishly Arthur's court when they come to inspect the wonders of his realm. To this point the pattern is clear.

Suddenly, however, the narrative curves away from the pattern both of the myth and of *Erec et Enide*, which it had to this point paralleled closely. Gawain urges Yvain not to join those who "degenerate after marriage," but to "increase his fame"(212) by continuing his career in the tournaments. From the point of view of the myth and of *Erec et Enide* the advice is well taken; Yvain does indeed stand to lose, as did Erec, both his reputation and his wife by yielding to Luxuria. But the terms upon which Gawain offers a new life are distorted and inadequate. There is neither gain nor merit in devotion to chivalric exercise for its own sake, tournaments in which the only possible gain is reputation and the only virtue undirected prowess. Yvain, too, has his work cut out for him; Laudine married him only to find a defender for the fountain. Yvain, however, departs with Gawain for a year of tournaments armed with Laudine's ring (his second such token; Lunette had also given him a magic ring), which will keep him safe as long as he remembers the giver. But he does not remember the giver, and the year passes.

At this point, as Woods points out, occurs the same sort of "unmotivated" action that marks *Erec et Enide*:

"Thus is revealed the familiar pattern—the hero has achieved great happiness and worldly success. In addition to his loving and beautiful wife, he gains such knightly success in the tourneys that Arthur and the other knights visit his tent, rather than he visiting theirs. At that pinnacle of fame and fortune, the unnamed messenger maiden enters and her reproving voice is the equivalent of the voice of God's messenger to Guillaume [in *William of England*] and Enide's accusing voice to Erec."[20] Woods' discontent with the sequence of events lies generally with the facts that since there is no obstacle "in the way of Yvain's return home except Laudine's anger at him for his broken pledge, he could have gone to the fountain at any point in the poem and made it rain so hard that she would have to take him back, for she had no other defender of her magic fountain"[21] and that "in the *Yvain* nothing is said about recovering Laudine's affection or his earlier status"; in fact, Yvain's first steps towards rehabilitation are "unconscious" since he is well-nigh mad. Thus, Woods concludes, "the motivation for the *Yvain* is also ambiguous and hardly comprehensible on the plot level alone."

But if the *matière* of the *Yvain* is at this point "ambiguous and hardly comprehensible," on the level of *sens* it seems clear enough. Like Erec, Yvain has failed to understand the nature of his preliminary triumph and has abandoned his quest midway. Erec refused to return from his withdrawal with Enide to the world from which he had set out; Yvain returns prematurely without having realized or even having considered the terms upon which his return is possible. He returns bearing a token of his accomplishment, Laudine's ring, but he does not use it properly, and it must in time be snatched from him.

The point is surely the same in the two poems. Love, the love of a lady, is the life and heart of the new twelfth-century chivalry: if love is wrongly used, knighthood degenerates into Luxuria; if it is ignored and forgotten, knighthood becomes the mere muscle-flexing of the first knights. Rightly used, love (marriage really), becomes the saving grace of the system because it directs the knight toward a set of aims and objects outside himself. Erec in his final adventures fought for others, and this is precisely the point of Yvain's rehabilitation. He must "return" to Laudine and through her to the proper world of knightly duty even as Erec had to "return" in a sense to his first relation with Enide and thence, on new terms, to the world of Arthur's court.

There is no need to analyze in detail these last adventures; Professor Julian Harris has done that and has pointed out how Yvain, having become "morally undermined" through his "excessive pride in worldly fame," moves, again like Erec, from a kind of unconscious desire for salvation, what Professor Harris calls "the latent capacity to redeem himself," through a series of increasingly altruistic adventures to a full realization of the place of the Christian knight in society,[22] to a point at which he has earned the right to return to Laudine and assume his place in the world.

Toward the end of his analysis of the *Yvain*, Professor Harris remarks that this romance is an "anti-Lancelot,"[23] and indeed the poem perhaps is best seen in its relationship to Chrétien's own unfinished *Lancelot* or *The Knight of the Cart*, the romance which immediately precedes it.[24] This romance cannot rightly be considered on the same terms as the rest of Chrétien's work since, as the poet himself states, both its *matière* and its *sens* were given to him by Marie de Champagne, he putting into it only the "pains and thought" of its execution. Also, Chrétien did not himself finish the work.

Even if, however, this telltale dedication did not exist,

I think it possible that the structure and tone of *Lancelot* are proof enough of Chrétien's intent in the poem. For certainly the poem is concerned with Chrétien's principal subject—the "conflicting claims of love, morality, and knightly honor"[25]—and it follows the plot structure that the poet previously had followed in *Erec et Enide*, though not, unfortunately, in *Cliges*, his next romance.

At the risk of digressing, I think we might say at this point a few words about *Cliges*, a poem usually judged, and rightly so, to be the least successful and the least interesting of Chrétien's extant romances. It is, in my view, an unsuccessful structural and thematic experiment. The story falls into two well-defined sections, the break occurring almost precisely one third of the way along. This obvious division has provided a basis for most of the statements of theme and intent which critics have made concerning the poem, statements which for the most part follow Professor Foerster's assumption that since the poem is quite obviously influenced by some version of the Tristan story, its structure and theme must of course follow that of the *Tristan*.

Yet such is not necessarily the case. It seems much more likely that Chrétien in *Cliges* is attempting, as he had done in *Erec et Enide* and would do later in *Lancelot*, to define the relationship between love and knighthood. However, instead of utilizing the single, though segmented, plot structure of the *Erec*, he attempts in *Cliges* to work through a double plot that, unfortunately, turns out to be no more than two stories clumsily tacked together. But despite the faulty workmanship, Chrétien's intentions are clear in *sens*, if not in *matière*. The two halves of the story—the romances of Alexander and Soredamors and of Cliges and Fenice—are plainly meant to contrast and in doing so to form an image of proper and improper chivalric love.

The first part of *Cliges*, dealing with the love of

Cliges's parents, Alexander and Soredamors, is a chivalric romance extolling, as Professor Foerster says,[26] the bourgeois ideal of married love. It is manifestly *not* derived from the Tristan story, nor from any other single work. Rather it is, as J. D. Bruce says, an "invention," a "combination of widely separated details,"[27] which strongly advocates chastity, modesty, and marriage along with the more usual chivalric virtues.

The second part of the romance clearly is modeled on the *Tristan* and stands, I think, in marked contrast to the first. Here, the heroine, Fenice, avoids consummating her marriage with the evil Prince Alis by means of a potion and spends the greater part of the poem in the arms of Cliges, her lover. Thus, while Fenice avoids the sin of Iseult by not yielding to both husband and lover, she most certainly is not spotless, and her frequently expressed fear that she will be identified with Iseult carries little conviction. For despite her protestations and those of Frappier, who regards her as a moral "perfectionist,"[28] Chrétien makes clear the carnal nature of her relationship with Cliges, and it is noteworthy that in the end he insists upon the marriage of the lovers, albeit he qualifies the union by defining it in terms of courtly rather than Christian standards.

What I am suggesting, at the risk perhaps of making Chrétien seem more didactical than he actually is, is that the two parts of the poem are meant to form a contrast of love affairs in which the courtly arrangement is intended to suffer. True, Chrétien does not specifically praise Alexander and Soredamors, nor specifically condemn Cliges and Fenice. He could not, given the conditions of his employment as a court poet, be expected to do so. But he does, I think, make clear in the structure and tone of the poem his thematic intentions, his *sens*, though he does so at the expense of *matière*.

Such a view of *Cliges* does much to illuminate *The*

Knight of the Cart, which follows it. For here Chrétien, despite the wishes of Marie de Champagne, reproduces both the tone and *sens* of *Cliges* to produce an anti-Lancelot *manqué,* a poem that in spite of the fact that Chrétien never finished it manages to convey a strong indictment of unredeemed courtly love. The tale in which Lancelot, rescuing the abducted Guinevere, rides in a hangman's cart and is later rebuked by the queen for hesitating to do so is too familiar to justify even casual summary. Again, as in *Erec et Enide* and *Yvain,* the poem falls into two main divisions. The first episode, which as Heinrich Zimmer pointed out follows very closely the archetypal heroic pattern,[29] is the rescue of Guinevere proper, and it is in this section that Marie's hand can be most clearly traced. Its culmination is the anger of Guinevere and the triumph of the courtly relationship in her rebuke of Lancelot, an incident presumably of great interest to the poet's audience.

The second episode, Lancelot's liaison with the queen and its consequences, is much more in Chrétien's characteristic vein and serves as a commentary on the poem's first action. For these incidents—the humiliations and, at times, almost ridiculous trials of the hero, the seduction, accusations, lies and half-lies, the imprisonment, the trial —are the true effects of the immoral courtly relationship presented in the first part of the poem. Represented here, in mythical terms, as in the *Erec* and the *Yvain,* is a failure to utilize properly the knowledge gained in the quest. Lancelot has overcome successfully the trials of the journey, but he fails to capitalize on his victory. In accepting, against his own hard-won judgment, Guinevere's estimate of the Meleagant situation and in agreeing to Guinevere's plan of action, in yielding to the courtly point of view, Lancelot refuses to "return" to the real world, infinitely preferring his withdrawal in the unreal world of courtly love. Like Erec, he is overcome by Luxuria, and like Yvain, he forgets the proper uses of love.

It is noteworthy in this connection that Chrétien's own part of the story ends in tragedy, with Lancelot imprisoned for the second time by Meleagant.[30] One might almost surmise that this ending represents Chrétien's judgment of his hero; it is a fitting end for an adulterous pair, both condemned by their crime, and is instructive that, unlike Erec and Yvain, Lancelot never returns from the fairy world of Meleagant to the reality those other heroes gained by struggle.

This examination of the structure of the romances of Chrétien de Troyes perhaps has led me away from what should have been the central issue of this discussion—the knight of the first romances. But what I have been trying to say is really simple enough: that in spite of the apparent aimlessness that most obviously separates the romantic from the epic quest, the romance, at least in Chrétien, has its own structural pattern and the desultory quest of the knight errant its own *raison d'être*, his discovery of the uses of his victories in the forests of Logres. That this structural pattern and theme are best explained by myth is both inconsequential and of great importance— inconsequential in that one need not perceive the myth to understand the romances; of great importance in that the myth is a demonstration of the validity of what the romance has to say.

But one must not only identify the myth; he must also use it, bring it to bear directly upon the literary work at hand for comparative and interpretive purposes. Analysis is never enough, however compendious, accurate, and useful it may be. Professor Patch's great compilation of otherworld tales[31] stops short of the mark by failing to relate myth to theme, though indeed without such guides we should each have to bring order out of chaos. But the myth is no more than a vehicle; what it is is less important than what it says. The romances of Chrétien say that love properly conceived and followed is the basis of chivalric virtue and true knighthood and, contrariwise, that love falsely conceived and followed is the destruction of knightly society.

Thus, the romances of Chrétien are not concerned so much with the winning of the lady, or with, mythically, the crossing of the threshold into the other world and the trials of the hero there, as with love's uses in this world. And though they are far removed from the primitive rites of savages, they mark also the progress from childhood to adulthood, from Yin to Yang. In no better way can I demonstrate Chrétien's concern with the uses of love than by comparing two of his romances briefly with their Welsh counterparts in *The Mabinogion*—the *Yvain* with *The Lady of the Fountain* and *Erec et Enide* with *Geraint and Enid*.

Since it is now admitted that Chrétien's romances and the *Mabinogion* have a common source, it may be instructive to note the general differences between these stories and to see what these may tell us about their differences in intention and theme. For example, J. D. Bruce has discussed differences in the motives of Erec and Geraint in abandoning their leisurely lives and in subjecting their wives to hardship and humiliation. The Welsh "hero's conduct in *Geraint and Enid* is expressly stated to be jealousy; in Chrétien's romance we are left to infer for ourselves what it is."[32] Regardless of what conclusions one draws from the difference, the difference itself, surely a major crux in the interpretation of the two romances, becomes an important clue in revealing the *sens* behind the *matière*.

The several structural differences between *Erec et Enide* and *Geraint and Enid* reveal Chrétien's concern with the later portions of the story, the "return" of Erec to the proper world of chivalric action. The Welsh story, on the other hand, is concerned with the first adventures— with the insults of the rude dwarf, the defeat of the Knight of the Sparrowhawk, and the return of Geraint in triumph to Arthur's court. The later incidents (based in the Welsh tale simply on Geraint's desire to test Enid's loyalty) are done in summary fashion; they have little point in themselves and they exhibit no clearly defined progression or sequence. This last section of *Geraint and Enid* reaches its climax after the Count Limouris (Count Oringle) adventure when Geraint recognizes his folly in suspecting his wife and so abandons his adventures. There is in the Welsh tale no hint of the developing search for self-knowledge which gives point and structure to Chrétien's romance.

Yvain and *The Lady of the Fountain* reveal much the same differences when seen side by side. Here again, the emphases of the two tales are reversed. Chrétien gets through the initial episodes as hastily as he can in order to get to what interests him, the redemption of Yvain. The Welsh poet, on the other hand, dwells on these early adventures and clearly regards the final series of combats merely as a group of supplementary wonders. And the detail of plot manipulation in the two confirms such a generalization. There is nothing in *The Lady of the Fountain* to match Gawain's appeal to Yvain to return to Arthur's court lest he lose his reputation. Yvain's vanity, which thus becomes in Chrétien the cause of Yvain's downfall, simply is missing from the Welsh story. Missing also from *The Lady of the Fountain* is the carefully conceived and maintained progression in the final incidents that mark the stages of Yvain's return to sanity and the fountain; these incidents are presented skillfully enough in the Welsh and with all the appropriate paraphernalia, including the lion, but in no clear thematic order.

I have restricted my entire analysis to Chrétien and deliberately have refrained from mentioning even his most immediate followers. He has no predecessors, of course, outside of the oral tradition and perhaps in romances of antiquity. It is exactly here, in their use of the oral tradition, that the difference between Chrétien and his successors in the romance tradition are most apparent. For supposing that both are using, in whatever form, the old traditional stories, it is Chrétien who almost alone sees and develops the possibilities for meaning inherent in the actions of the new knight, the gallant knight of the quest. In the romances of Chrétien's successors, the pattern is followed faithfully and the quest duly fulfilled; the actions of the *rite de passage* are described faithfully. But the child-knight remains a child and the symbols with which the adventures abound reflect nothing beyond themselves.

For example, all of the studies devoted to the romance make it clear that a great many romances use the "otherworld" story, which contains in form if not in meaning almost all the superficial features of the hero quest—the messenger, the barrier, the magic garden realm, the astonishing adventures. *Le Bel Inconnu*, which follows the assumed date of Chrétien's death by only a few years, and *La Mule Sanz Frain*, written only a few years later, illustrate the motif of the hero's journey into a strange land, his adventures there, and his return bearing a token of his triumph, a blonde fairy wife or a bridle. Yet despite the obvious influence of Chrétien upon both poets and upon all writers of the genre and despite the fact that these later writers are utilizing exactly the same sort of source material available to Chrétien, the authors of these two romances, while mimicking the pattern of the hero's quest and copying faithfully the sentiments and even the attitudes of their great model, fail to perceive and hence to communicate to their readers the hard core of meaning inherent in Chrétien's adaptations.

And I have picked the best, or at least the most coherent, examples of the French chivalric romance. As the genre develops in the thirteenth century, in pieces like *Meraugis de Portlesguez, Le Vengeance de Raguidel, Gliglois,* and the others even the pattern is lost in a maze of mere questing, in endless recitals of adventures, in a catalogue of wonders put down without regard to sequence.

To return to the archetypal knight, Chrétien, working out of an unknown body of Celtic legend, reflects and creates a knight startlingly different from the knights of the Crusades and *chansons de geste.* He is the knight of the new literary chivalry, no longer a man motivated by barbaric concepts of political acquisition and baronial war and defined principally by his faith in his own military prowess. Converted by love, he now makes his way about the countryside, a seeker of marvels, a defender of the weak, and an enemy of evil.

Chrétien does, however, show the evolution of these new values, does illuminate by means of the monomyth the process by which a knight comes to discover how love may transform simple adventure into purposeful action on behalf of others. In *Erec et Enide,* in *Yvain,* and, conversely, in *Cliges* and *Lancelot,* a knight through love becomes something more than an adventurer; he becomes for the first time a gentleman. Far from being episodic tales of marvels and prowess, Chrétien's romances are among the first and greatest of the novels which, like *Great Expectations* and *The Ambassadors* and *The Portrait of the Artist as a Young Man,* recount the process of self-realization and human discovery.

THE STAINED KNIGHT

SIR GAWAIN AND THE GREEN KNIGHT

IT IS a miracle of literature that the romances end in triumph. For, as we have seen in Chrétien's *Lancelot,* the seeds of psychological conflict and tragedy are built into the fabric of the romance as they were into knighthood and courtly life, and it is perhaps indicative of the tastes of the courtly audience that while the experiences and trials of courtly love continue as the dominant theme of the romance, its dilemmas seldom appear. A cursory examination of the most popular romances of the period—*Escanor, Claris et Laris, Floriant et Florete, Gawain et Humbaut, Gliglois*—reveals an almost total dedication to the doctrines and rites of the religion of love, and even in those romances which do not involve adultery, a casual sensuality underlies the soft surface of adventure.[1] It is significant, I think, that the romancers of this period make so little of this conflict of love and honor. Something—their own inclinations or the taste or moral climate of the period—prevented their exploiting such an apparent and significant theme in what one would think to be the most sympathetic and flexible of genres.

In the romances I have named, virtue (or at least marriage) is at last triumphant; as Fr. Gervase Mathew says, by the late fourteenth century, certainly a union of the chivalric ideals of courtly love and the bourgeois ideal of marriage had taken place.[2] This is, of course, an easy and natural transition from the earlier adulterous union, accomplished with almost no literary fuss or strain. The adultery of early romances such as *Flamenca*, *Joufrois*, and *Châtelain de Coucy* disappears from the genre; Cliges and Tristan become almost imperceptibly Palamon and Arveragus. Actual knighthood was by now all but obsolete,[3] though its memory was still green. Sociologically, the middle class was approaching its coming of age in the Renaissance and Reformation, and the growing influence of Mr. Doolittle's "middle-class morality" was apparent.

Yet, just as Chrétien had seen and to a degree developed the enormous possibilities for conflict in the relations of knight and lady, so here nearly at the end of the romance tradition two writers, working in different literary modes, reveal in two of the major poems of their age the same tragic conflict which Chrétien had revealed in his portion of *Lancelot* and which had lain almost untouched since his time.

The first, Chaucer's *Troilus and Criseyde*, presents the dilemma of the courtly lover and lady in stark terms. However one takes the final lines—which record Chaucer's involvement and do not affect the clear point of the poem —the tragedy of the lovers is the direct result of the code to which they have committed themselves. To be sure, Criseyde is "slyding of corage" and Troilus innocent almost beyond belief and the tragedy is to a degree brought on by the characters of the lovers. But Chaucer, influenced by Boethius and the doctrine of Fortune's wheel and involved in the dilemma of whether to be a clerk of Venus or a clerk of Christ, attributes the double sorrow of the lovers to the irreconcilable conflicts inherent in courtly love. Troilus and Criseyde cannot remain lovers because their kind of love, clandestine and immoral, can exist only in the popularized romance of the earlier period or in the hothouse environment of the Provençal court. Comes a crisis in Logres or Troy or England and courtly love disintegrates before the realities of everyday life and passions. Troilus is right in begging Criseyde to flee with him; it is in fact their only hope, and Criseyde's decision to preserve the secrecy of their relationship, abiding by the prescription of the code, reveals the cause of their destruction.

Sir Gawain and the Green Knight presents the corollary of this theme, the effect of courtly love upon society, under another guise; it is almost a totally different kind of poem, though both are technically romances. Where the *Troilus* is direct, dramatic, and straightforward, *Sir Gawain and the Green Knight* is allusive, symbolic, and cyclic. *Sir Gawain and the Green Knight* is in the manner of Chrétien and is the last great flowering of that tradition; *Troilus and Criseyde* is indebted heavily to Boccaccio and the new narrative technique and is the forerunner of the novel.

But each poem deals in its own way with the immorality and, hence, the tragedy of courtly love rather than with its joys. Neither Troilus nor Gawain is wholly commendable, and the conduct of both Criseyde and Bercilak's Lady is inspired, finally, by elements in their nature considerably more primitive and more deceptive than those recognized by Andreas Capellanus.

The great theme of the two poems is the failure of courtly love to bring the promised joy of its first rapturous days. What is implied in *The Knight of the Cart*, that the only possible end of *fin amor* is degradation and tragedy, is made starkly manifest in *Troilus and Criseyde* and symbolically persuasive in *Sir Gawain and the Green Knight*. And what had been the personal tragedy of a single knight in Chrétien becomes in *Sir Gawain and the Green Knight* the failure of a whole social order.

It is not surprising, therefore, to find that *Sir Gawain and the Green Knight* has been examined in great detail in terms of the morality of its hero, and whether we agree with a recent critic who maintains that the purpose of the poem "is to show what a splendid man Gawain is"[4] or with an even more recent one who accuses Gawain of the "irony of muddled conscience,"[5] the poem's moral concern with the degree of Gawain's guilt—and in the poem this is a specifically Christian moral concern—is immediately apparent and everywhere persuasive.

In recent years there has been also an even more insistent strain in the critical activity centering on the poem; the myth critics, following the lead of such early workers as Miss Weston, Nitze, and Krappe, have shaped and defined the poem's essential structure and symbolism in terms of Celtic sun gods and vegetation myths. Thus the celebrated analyses of Heinrich Zimmer[6] and John Speirs[7] have succeeded in revealing a number of layers of meaning in the poem; to Zimmer the poem reveals man's conquest of death and to Speirs the annual death and rebirth of nature seen in the vegetation myth of the Green Man.[8]

The poem thus involves both a moral and a myth, both test and quest, and it is my argument here that the great moral theme of the poem—the failure of chivalric morality—can best be discerned in its structure and, more specifically, in its picture of the knightly quest.

Clearly, Gawain's task is spiritual rather than physical. It is usual to state, of course, that almost any given quest in the medieval romance is undertaken in behalf of a worthy cause and so has as its aim a nonphysical and thus "spiritual" goal. But aside from such obvious exceptions as the Grail quest in the Arthurian cycle and the quests of Chrétien's penitent knights the quest is undertaken primarily for the secular ideal of chivalric duty and not from any purely religious or spiritual motives. However, the quest of Gawain in this poem, although emanating from the chivalric virtue of loyalty to one's oath, is described in such terms as to transform it into a semi-religious quest for a spiritual object or set of values.

The journey of Gawain to the domain of the Green Knight is, in mythical terms, a *rite de passage* by which Gawain is initiated into a full understanding of himself and his code of values and, by way of that knowledge, to an understanding of the true nature of the chivalry of Arthur's court. Certainly the initiatory rite, as seen by Van Gennep[9] and the other commentators, is reflected in the poem; Gawain, having received what Joseph Campbell designates a "call to adventure,"[10] journeys forth from his usual world (Arthur's court) and retires into a strange land where he undergoes various tests (the assaults of the Lady) and receives a gift of great value to his people (the green girdle). He returns bearing this saving gift, but is scorned and is unable to redeem his people using this curative device. It is important also that the two confrontations of Gawain with the Green Knight should occur during the festival of the New Year, the time when initiatory rites of savages are performed[11] and also when the "annulling of the sins and faults of an individual and of those of the community as a whole"[12] (which is, as we shall see, the object of Morgan le Fay's plan) is accomplished through rites symbolizing the "cosmogenic moment of the fight between the god and the primordial dragon."[13] The application of these general features of the *rite de passage* to the poem will become clearer in detailed analysis.

Gawain's quest plainly is intended to be taken as a spiritual task. As Professor Denver Baughan points out, Arthur is not able to qualify for the adventure; he can only swing the Green Knight's axe wildly about, unable to strike with it.[14] Gawain alone can deal the blow effectively. The element of magic in the poem reinforces this interpretation; the beheading game is from the beginning no ordinary chivalric adventure. Since this is true, it is likewise clear that Gawain's search for the Green Chapel becomes a spiritual quest. Note that Gawain can find the castle of Bercilak only after he has prayed that he find "some lodging wherein to hear mass" (755)[15] and that he discovers the castle *immediately* upon ending the prayer with the words "Christ's cross me speed" (762). Gawain's journey becomes, in a sense, the journey of the individual toward a spiritual ideal higher than himself, made alone through the valley of the shadow with "no soul but the Savior to speak to" (696). Gawain's quest is also shown through imagery to be essentially religious. The pentangle device on Gawain's arms is described in great detail and in religious terms (619-69). He is said to undertake the journey "for God's sake" (692). Few people live in the wilderness through which Gawain rides "who loved God or their fellows with good heart" (702). Gawain prays to Mary on his journey (737-39), and it is clear that Gawain is under the Virgin's special protection (1769) and that his fate is in the hands of God (1967, 2135-39). Gawain twice says that in keeping his tryst with the Green Knight he is obedient to God's will (2156-59, 2208-11) and in his final interview with Bercilak, Gawain receives what sounds like religious absolution from the Green Knight (2390-94).[16]

The *Gawain*-poet has constructed also a clear series of parallel incidents within the poem in order to compare two levels of courtesy and chivalry, that of Arthur's court and that of Bercilak's castle. In the beginning, Arthur's company receives high praise:

> In greatest well-being   abode they together:
> The knights whose renown   was next to the Savior's,
> The loveliest ladies   who ever were living,
> And he who held court,   the most comely of kings.
> For these fine folk were yet   in their first flush of youth
> Seated there. . . .   (49-54)

Guinevere is:

> The comeliest was the Queen,
> With dancing eyes of grey.
> That a fairer he had seen
> No man might truly say.   (81-84)

Certainly there is no sign of corruption or bad blood here. But when we compare these descriptions of Arthur's court with the later descriptions of Bercilak's court, it becomes apparent that Bercilak's court is just as elaborate as Arthur's and in several major respects closer to the courtly and chivalric ideal. First the Lady of the castle:

> In face she was fairest   of all, and in figure,
> In skin and in color,   all bodily qualities;
> *Lovelier Gawain thought,   even than Guinevere.*
>   (943-45, my italics)

Second, Bercilak's court boasts the finer hospitality. Compare Arthur's welcoming of the Green Knight, who has said that he comes in peace (see 264-70):

> ". . . Sir courteous knight,
> If battle here you crave,
> You shall not lack a fight."   (275-77)

with the Green Knight's welcoming of the armed Gawain:

> "I'll truly as long   as I live be the better
> That Gawain at God's   own feast was my guest."
> (1034-35)

Arthur, we note, is almost rude and certainly high-handed, since the unarmed Green Knight has said nothing about fighting and, in fact, carries the holly branch of peace (205, 265). On the other hand, Gawain, armed to the teeth, is accepted as a guest and the modest court is delighted to have him (916-19).

It can be shown, moreover, that this contrast between Arthur's court and Bercilak's court furnishes the real motivation for the Green Knight's challenge. In his final explanation, Bercilak tells Gawain that he was sent to Arthur's court by Morgan:

> "To make trial of your pride,   and to see if the people's
> Tales were true   of the Table's great glory."
> (2457-58)

He announces to Arthur upon his arrival at Camelot that he cannot remain long:

> "But, sir, since thy name   is so nobly renowned,
> Since thy city the best   is considered, thy barons
> The stoutest in steel gear   that ride upon steeds,
> Of all men in the world   the most worthy and brave,
> Right valiant to play with   in other pure pastimes,
> Since here, I have heard,   is the highest of courtesy—
> Truly, all these things   have brought me at this time."
> (257-63)

Thus, since the test of the courtesy and chivalry of the Round Table causes the exchange of blows, the differences between the two courts, seen in conjunction with the spiritual nature of the quest, become important in determining the theme of the poem.

In an important three-fold parallel, moreover, the Green Knight and his Lady heap aspersions upon the courtesy and chivalry of Arthur's court by exposing it to irony. First, when none of the knights of the Round Table rises to meet his challenge, the Green Knight says:

> "What!" quoth the hero, "Is this Arthur's household,
> The fame of whose fellowship fills many kingdoms?
> Now where is your vainglory? Where are your victories?
> Where is your grimness, your great words, your anger?"
> (308-11)

Second, when Gawain is adamant in resisting the overtures of the Lady, she doubts that the man before is the courtly Gawain of whose *gentilesse* she has heard:

> "He who blesses all words reward this reception!
> I doubt if indeed I may dub you Gawain."
>
> . . . . . .
>
> "One as good as is Gawain the gracious considered,
> (And courtly behavior's found wholly in him)
> Not lightly so long could remain with a lady
> Without, in courtesy, craving a kiss
> At some slight subtle hint at the end of a story."
> (1291-92, 1296-1300)

Third, when Gawain flinches at the Green Knight's first feint, Bercilak says:

> "Not Gawain thou art who so good is considered,
> Ne'er daunted by host in hill or in dale;
> Now in fear, ere thou feelest a hurt, thou are flinching;
> Such cowardice never I knew of that knight."
> (2270-73)

It would seem that the Green Knight, like his Lady, finds something wanting in the courtesy and the chivalry of the Round Table. In each case these ironical thrusts follow passages in which the Green Knight and his Lady have heaped extravagant praise upon the Round Table and upon Gawain. Thus, it would seem that the difference between the two courts is further reinforced by having Bercilak and the Lady first praise the chivalry of the court of Arthur and then, having tested it by their own standards, find fault with it.

It is thus clear that even in the heyday of the Round Table, as seen in *Sir Gawain and the Green Knight*, there are disturbing elements which it will be best to list for the sake of clarity:

1. The Arthurian court generally, and Gawain in particular, are subjected at crucial moments to a searching irony which they cannot answer except by raging (316-21, 2284-85).

2. Arthur plainly is incapable of responding to the Green Knight's challenge (329-30), and although Gawain is the only knight capable of undertaking the quest, yet even he succeeds only partly in resisting the temptations set before him and so returns to the court, his victory tainted with dishonor.

3. Guinevere is singled out for attack by Morgan (2456-62), and she clearly suffers by comparison with Bercilak's Lady (943-45).

4. Most puzzling of all, Morgan le Fay, whatever her design, fails, for Guinevere, whom Morgan wished to kill by fear, remains alive.

If we assume that the *Gawain*-poet knew the legend in its entirety,[18] we will be able, I think, to fit these pieces of evidence into a meaningful pattern.

Morgan, a former mistress and student of the friendly magician Merlin (2448-51), is attempting to reform

Arthur's court,[19] to test the pride and the reputation of the Round Table by exposing it to the irony of a civilization more courtly and chivalrous, represented by Bercilak. Morgan's plan for reform includes an exchange of blows, a knightly game, followed by a series of temptations designed to test the spiritual qualities of the company. Arthur, presumably because of his pride, cannot even qualify for the test, and only Gawain, because of his modesty the best of the knights (353-54), can meet the challenge. Gawain embarks then upon an initiatory spiritual quest, a *rite de passage*, undergoes the necessary dangers and temptations, and returns bearing with him the green girdle, ironically a symbol both of his success and of his failure. Though Gawain's mission is not completely successful, it would seem that Morgan's plan had succeeded since Gawain has supplied the court with a strong object lesson in the value of chastity and faithfulness. Yet this is obviously not so since Guinevere, whose death was an integral part of the plan, still lives. Then too Gawain goes into an extended antifeminist harangue, presumably aimed at Bercilak's Lady (2414-28). Yet we know that the responsibility for the failure lies solely with Gawain, that he accepted the girdle to save his own life, and that the Lady, far from being an evil temptress, was acting out a part written for her by Morgan and is even more gracious than Guinevere. The antifeminist discourse must be aimed at Guinevere.

The point, I think, is this. Morgan's testing of Gawain is designed to warn the court of two potential dangers, sexual wantonness and unfaithfulness. Wantonness is personified by Guinevere, who, we remember, is later to bring about the downfall of the court by her affair with Lancelot. Unfaithfulness, a breach in the chivalric code of loyalty, is manifested in the court, which later will indulge in personal feuds culminating in the treachery of

Mordred. Morgan's plan fails on both counts because Arthur, though humiliated, is able to comfort and protect the queen (470-75), and Gawain, though able to resist the temptations of the Lady, cannot keep complete faith with Bercilak. Both dangers remain in the court, and it is obvious from the knights' laughter (2513-18) that the court does not take seriously the green girdle, the gift of great value, which is also a warning. Only the initiated Gawain perceives the danger.

The *Gawain*-poet, I maintain, is presenting us, within a deliberately limited form, a semi-allegorical presentation of the whole history and meaning of the Round Table. Morgan attempts reform; Gawain fails in keeping faith with Bercilak; treacherous Guinevere remains alive. The form of the poem is thus consciously limited in time and space to facilitate a unified and complete presentation of the progress of the Round Table; only in a single, complete adventure could the poet achieve a unified design which would reflect the whole of the tragedy. In this sense the poem is semi-allegorical in method; we are not presented with a segment of the action, but with a miniature version of the whole action. The gay light tone, which reflects the ignorance and pride of Arthur's court, is maintained throughout the scenes taking place within the safe precincts of Camelot, but as the poem moves to the outside world, the tone changes radically. The journeys are always difficult and dangerous, the terrain rugged and foreboding. The scene of the final encounter, the Green Chapel, is, to Gawain, the "cursedest chapel" that he ever saw (2196). The prevailing tone is that of Christmas, but we must remember that the court is in "their first flush of youth" and that all the knights are ironically ignorant of Morgan's attempts to forestall the fate which will overtake them and of the dangers outside the court, a part of any spiritual quest. Only the returned

Gawain, who has himself made the initiatory journey, sees the imminent destruction which he expresses in his condemnation of women and which he attempts to delay by the institution of the green baldric.

The presence of some such purpose behind the romantic facade of the poem is further demonstrable by an examination of those features of the poem which the *Gawain*-poet adds to his source materials. Professor Kittredge lists those elements which were "certainly added or greatly elaborated by the English author" as:

the learned introductory stanza summarizing the fabulous settlements of Western Europe . . . ; the description of the Christmas festivities (i, 3) and that of the Green Knight (i, 7-9); the challenge (i, 12-13) and the speech of Gawain (i, 16); the highly poetical stanzas on the changing seasons (ii, 1-2); the very elaborate description of the process of arming a knight (ii, 4-6), with the allegorical account of the pentangle of virtues (ii, 7); Gawain's itinerary,—Logres, North Wales, Anglesea, Holyhead, the wilderness of Wirral (ii, 9); the winter piece (ii, 10); the justly celebrated account of the three hunts (iii, 1ff.).[20]

The first of these additions, the introductory stanza, serves to introduce (1) the theme of treachery in the allusion to Antenor and (2) more importantly, the theme of change, of the alternation of happiness and sorrow in the history of England:

> War, waste, and wonder there
> Have dwelt within its bound;
> And bliss has changed to care
> In quick and shifting round.   (16-19)

This theme of the alternation of "bliss" and "care" is immediately reinforced:

And after this famous knight   founded his Britain,
Bold lords were bred there,   delighting in battle,
Who many times dealt   in destruction. More marvels
Befell in those fields   since the days of their finding
Than anywhere else   upon earth that I know of.

                                           (20-24)

In discussing Gawain's acceptance of the Green Knight's
challenge, the poet says:

In the hall glad was Gawain   those games to begin,
But not strange it would seem   if sad were the ending;
For though men having drunk much   are merry in mind,
Full swift flies a year,   never yielding the same,
The start and the close   very seldom according.

                                           (495-99)

Thus, at the beginning of the poem, the English poet
adds to his source materials passages which emphasize the
theme of change, the alternation of "bliss" and "care"
in the history of England. Seen in the light of Arthurian
history, these remarks of the poet seem perfectly applicable to a poem which deals with the court in "their first
flush of youth" ignorant of the treachery and civil war
which will indeed change its "bliss" to "care."

The "description of the Christmas festivities [at both
courts] (i, 3) and that of the Green Knight (i, 7-9); the
challenge [including the failure of Arthur] (i, 12-13) and
the speech of Gawain" were necessary if the poet was to
carry through his contrasting of the courts of Arthur and
Bercilak. For example, Christmas and New Year's Day,
called by the poet a second Christmas (64), seem to be
primarily social occasions at Arthur's court; while we have
references to the singing of carols (42) and to the "singing
of mass in the chapel" (62), there is no indication that
the season has any special religious significance to Arthur's

court; in fact, even Arthur's priests join in the general merriment (63). On the other hand, we get a full description of the solemn Christmas Evensong at Bercilak's castle including the observation that the knights "soberly sat through the service" (940). Moreover, Bercilak tells Gawain that he will be better off "that Gawain at God's own feast was [his] guest" (1035). In much the same way, the description of the Green Knight reinforces the contrast between the two courts by pointing out that Arthur immediately challenges the unarmed stranger to combat. Again, the challenge and Gawain's humble acceptance speech were added to emphasize Arthur's prideful attempt to deliver the blow, his consequent failure, and Gawain's humility in accepting and fulfilling the challenge.

The descriptions of the changing seasons may have been added (1) as unifying and transitional devices and (2) as a means of supplying imagery of natural flux and change which would remind the reader of the alternation of "bliss" and "care" introduced at the beginning of the poem. The description of the arming of Gawain may emphasize the contrast between the two courts by stressing Bercilak's kindly welcome to the armed Gawain. The description of Gawain's pentangle was added almost certainly to reinforce the spiritual quest theme. Finally, the descriptions of the journey and winter reinforce the contrast between the warmth of the court and the wildness outdoors, and the hunting scenes furnish parallels and commentaries on the temptations of Gawain, who has remained home from the hunt.

Professor Kittredge states also that the *denouement* of the poem, Gawain's return to Arthur's court, "shows plain traces of innovation."[21] Gawain's return to the court, "full of shame," is "contrary to custom, for the old French poets are loath to let Gawain come off from any adventure without the highest credit."[22] It seems that the poet wished this obviously nontraditional conclusion to be regarded seriously. It is important to the poem as a whole that our final view of Gawain should be that of an initiated and matured penitent rather than of a stainless conqueror. The poet states that the king and the court laughed loudly at the king's decision that all the knights wear green baldrics (2513-18); we are not told that Gawain laughed with them. This ending also relates Gawain's adventure to the whole Arthurian court and reinforces the theory that the poet is writing not simply an isolated adventure of Gawain but a highly compressed allegorical commentary on the entire Arthurian history.

If I am right, the *Gawain*-poet is using the myth of the hero's quest to develop a theme which lies at the core of medieval literature: that the tragedy of the Round Table, and of the secular society which it symbolizes, was inevitable, given its basis in *fin amor*, and that seeds of that tragedy were present even in the "first flush of youth" of the joyous court at Christmas time.

And this theme is directly related to the development of the literary knight. For all his simplicity, Roland is an unqualified hero of the epic tradition; Chrétien's *Lancelot*, coming at the very beginning of the new romance tradition and the development of the courtly lover-knight, contains, though it does not develop, the seeds of the courtly dilemma; the failure of Gawain in this later fourteenth-century romance demonstrates the effects of Lancelot's sin and foreshadows the imminent downfall of the chivalric system in literature as well as in life. For although Gawain and Lancelot could have escaped the general guilt and destruction of the court, they did not choose to do so. In accepting the green baldric, Gawain is reunited to the court; but his experience at Bercilak's court, his hard-won lesson in the morality of chivalry, like Lancelot's, is of no use. Like Erec and Yvain, he returns bearing the saving gift from beyond the forest, but he allows the green girdle to become the green baldric without protest and so, unlike Erec and Yvain, is willing to accept again the false standards of Arthur's court, renouncing the values that might have saved both himself and his entire society.

Thus, the *Gawain*-poet ,like Chrétien, uses the knightly quest as an image of man's quest for the elixir of life, capable, if properly used, of redeeming him and his society. In Chrétien the gift is love, and although Erec and Yvain, through struggle and pain having discovered the importance of love in a chivalric society, emerge with an enlightened view of knighthood, Lancelot succumbs to a false view of love, *l'amour courtois*, and so, at least in Chrétien's own romance, is last seen in the prison that Guinevere has created for him from her confusion of proper chivalric values and standards.

In *Sir Gawain and the Green Knight*, the essential conflict is more sharply etched; the failure that Chrétien saw as a contingency of knighthood the *Gawain*-poet sees, if not quite as a necessity (as Malory will see it), then as an almost unavoidable correlative of courtly life. Gawain cannot or does not communicate his lesson, though he tells his story; the warning to Arthur against wantonness and the breaking of faith go unspoken. In the end, Gawain's failure and humiliation go for nought, and the poem ends in the hollow laughter of the doomed court.

And if the great majority of romances which make up the bulk of the genre, like Arthur's court, reflect a cheery confidence in knighthood and its ideals, a confidence contrary to the shaken faith of *The Knight of the Cart* and *Sir Gawain and the Green Knight*, it is nonetheless these greater works that have touched upon the truth of the tragic consequences of chivalric life and so have continued to live.

THE PHILOSOPHICAL KNIGHT

THE CANTERBURY TALES

I⊤ ɪs impossible to date with any precision the decline of chivalry. Students disagree as to the time and place of its greatest flowering, and although this "Christian form of the military life"[1] constituted for nearly four centuries the social code by which the aristocracy of Europe lived, it is difficult to ascertain just when it "lost its moral aspect [if indeed it ever actually possessed it] and passed into aestheticism, became unmuscular and largely decorative."[2] It is certain, however, that as the historians[3] have shown, the institution of knighthood was under attack from the twelfth century onward for not living up to its own ideals. The reproaches of clerics and laymen alike demonstrate that, during these years, the "knights' love of ease and luxury, their cowardice, their arrogance, and their plundering activities"[4] contrasted sharply with their oaths of investiture and so sharply qualify Froissart's idealized portraits.

But in literature, if not in life, the knight continued heroic. While the most perceptive of the writers of romance, Chrétien and the *Gawain*-poet, see even in the idealized questing knight (who almost certainly never actually existed) the essential tragedy of life inherent in the confused standards of the archetypal courtly society, the great majority of the romancers presented, even in Chaucer's time, the idealized knight of popular tradition in the brightest primary colors. Proud, loyal, fearless, yet also devout, magnanimous, humble, merciful, courteous, and cultured—these traditional literary wonders ride about the countryside, seemingly unconscious of the paradoxes of morality and religion underlying their code of life.

Thus, the figure of the knight errant that Chaucer inherited was fixed in the courtly literary tradition. In fact, Chaucer's first major work, *The Book of the Duchess*, an elegy written on the death of Blanche of Lancaster, is thoroughly in the French courtly mode and is greatly indebted in substance, as well as in form and in tone, to the *Roman de la Rose*, Froissart, and, particularly, Machaut. The hero of the poem, "a wonder wel-farynge knyght" (452)[5] clothed in black, is discovered by the narrator-dreamer sitting mournfully against a tree. And the first striking feature of the knight is that he is a totally conventionalized figure. In fact, from the knight's physical attitude and first words:

> For-why he heng hys hed adoun,
> And with a dedly sorwful soun
> He made of rym ten vers or twelve
> Of a compleynte to hymselve,
> The moste pitee, the moste rowthe,
> That ever I herde. . . .   (461-66)

it is impossible to tell if he is suffering from the malady of love or from some more legitimate ailment; certainly the vocabulary ("dedly sorwful soun," a "compleynte to hymselve, / The moste pitee, the moste rowthe") and the mannerisms (the head "heng . . . adoun," "ful pitous

pale, and nothyng red") might suggest any number of
the highly artificial, highly stylized emotional situations
common in the romances as well as genuine grief. It is
only with the "compleynte" itself that we discover the
truth of the matter: "my lady bryght . . . / Is fro me
ded and ys agoon" (478-79).

The rest of the poem bears out this initial impression.
Throughout the long conversation that follows, the knight
never departs from his courtly behavior. During the
condemnation of fortune, the involved allegory of the
chess game, and the long recital of his courtship, the
knight's manner of speech does not change; whatever his
subject and emotion, his tone is measured and correct.
As Kittredge says, he is, unlike the dreamer, "not naïf
at all. On the contrary, he is an adept in the courtly
conventions, which have become a part of his manner of
thought and speech."[6] "The experience he describes [that
of a courtly love affair] is typical, and he speaks throughout in the settled language of the chivalric system."[7]

Chaucer's stiff and conventionalized characterization
of the knight could be attributed easily to a young writer's
inexperienced mimicry of his models. But the rest of the
poem, particularly the beautifully individualized narrator
—incredulous and confused by his weariness, his woeful
predicament in love, and his reading of the story of Ceyx
and Alcyone—demonstrates that Chaucer could from the
beginning write originally and imaginatively. The knight,
however, is deliberately stylized and in this kind of poem,
the courtly elegy, it would be entirely inappropriate to
individualize him. To change the knight's character or
even his mode of speech would be to alter the genre and
to mar the poem. Even Robert Louis Stevenson was not
free, we remember, to create a completely sympathetic
pirate. The narrator-dreamer was something else again;
being a part of the machinery of the poem and a *persona*

besides, he might reasonably be presented in a new way. But the knight in such a poem was unalterable.

Impossible not to note, even in such a relatively slight piece as *The Book of the Duchess,* is Chaucer's good taste, his instinctive "feel" with genre. Here in a conventional poem he obeys convention, knowing that in its stylized Frenchiness and conformity lay the poem's greatest charm. *Troilus and Criseyde* is another matter. Whether technically a romance or a tragedy—actually it is neither—Chaucer conceived it as a realistic work, and its knights—Troilus, Pandarus, Hector, Diomede, and the rest—are, for all their classic lineaments, sturdy, recognizable Englishmen. Thus there is room in this poem for the individualized, realistically drawn knights with whom the poet was not free to deal in *The Book of the Duchess.*

The *sens* is to a degree the same in both poems—the progress of love. But that theme is here viewed as having its basis in reality rather than in literary convention. The pangs of Troilus, observed through the lenses of tradition in *The Book of the Duchess,* are realized acutely in this later poem and accompanied by an analysis of motive— e.g., Troilus's natural shame at revealing his true condition to his comrades whose similar pains he had mocked; Pandarus's reluctance to involve his niece in what he knows to be an immoral affair overmatched by his incurable predilection for meddling—which does much to make lifelike the conventionalized behavior and dilemmas of courtly love.

Thus, the knights of *Troilus and Criseyde* are seen by Chaucer and by us not as literary types but as recognizable individuals caught in a tragic situation, trapped by a code of behavior which in itself contains the seeds of tragedy and involved in a poem which is both realistic and tragic. But, interestingly enough, no matter how steadily or how much as a whole Chaucer views the characters of *Troilus and Criseyde* as men and women, he seldom portrays them as knights and ladies. Their knightly occupations and status, their traditional battles and ceremonies, appear only peripherally and influence the action not at all. Except that courtly love is peculiar to a leisured courtly society and restricted by the chivalric code, the major characters of the poem need not have been knights and ladies at all.

This universality of character stems partly from the ancient setting. So much has been made, and rightly so, of the manner in which Chaucer renders as contemporary the sights, sounds, ideas, and values of antiquity that we sometimes forget that much of the effect of the poem— for example, the persuasive atmosphere of doom engendered by the inevitability of the fall of Troy—stems from the fact that its characters died long ago and have had time to become universal. As far as the poem as literature is concerned, this universality of character enhances rather than detracts from the appeal of the poem; we feel closer to Troilus and Criseyde than we do to Gawain and Bercilak's Lady. But only in *The Canterbury Tales* does Chaucer come to deal with the knight as knight. This is to be expected, given the scope and method of *The Canterbury Tales*. One of the purposes of the book is to describe society, its nature and structure, and what we would call "occupational groups" necessarily must be defined and fitted together. But Chaucer's interest in his "verray, parfit gentil knyght" (I, 72) surely lies deeper and extends further than a sociological survey of his era. *The Book of the Duchess* dealt with a literary convention, *Troilus and Criseyde* with a man and woman who happened also to be a knight and lady; *The Canterbury Tales* inherits both images of knighthood and adds to them a third. In *The Canterbury Tales* for the first time Chaucer deals with the knight in the context of his fourteenth-century knighthood.

The clause of the General Prologue devoted to characterization begins deliberately, indeed somewhat sententiously, with the Knight: "And at a knyght than wol I first bigynne" (I, 42). It is remarkable to see what the critics have made of the thirty-five lines which follow, almost half of which simply record the Knight's campaigns. We are told at one extreme that the Knight is meant to stand as an ideal not only of conventional but of actual knightly conduct, and at the other, that his very perfection constitutes a kind of parody of the actual knight with whom Chaucer would have been likely to associate.[8] Muriel Bowden, working out of Watriquet's *Dit*, takes the fact that the Knight is both "worthy" and "wys" (I, 68) to be a normal statement of the two faces of the chivalric coin:[9] R. M. Lumiansky, however, places great emphasis upon the "though" of "though that he were worthy, he was wys" and so finds an "unexpected element" in Chaucer's characterization: "this man is also notable for courteous conduct and piety, and these are not qualities regularly found in professional military men of any age."[10] Despite such variations in emphasis, however, certain qualities of the Knight would seem indisputable: he is one of the few pilgrims that Chaucer seems genuinely to admire; his motives in making the pilgrimage are purely and genuinely religious; most important, his values are essentially old-fashioned and conservative in an age of social transition.

The account of the Knight in the General Prologue is meant by Chaucer to be read against the background of the real state of chivalry with which the poet's courtly, though not necessarily blindly chivalric audience, was doubtless familiar. As sophisticated men and women, they knew well that the "feats of heroism in single combat" and the "crusades and adventures" had a hundred years before "lost [their] vitality."[11] Yet here Chaucer's portrait presents a man whose adventures are real indeed. Why else should Chaucer, noted for narrative economy, present us with a dazzling array of campaigns if not to convince his immediate audience and us of the reality, the non-conventionalized, non-stylized reality of the Knight's achievement. Again, Chaucer's audience would have been painfully aware that "the sophisticated [because no longer vital] chivalry of the age meant increasing pomp and display, which manifested itself in magnificent tournaments, elaborate banquets, colourful heraldry, and more splendid houses. Such rivalry and display was fostered by the chivalrous court of Edward III, with its cult of the Round Table, and the luxurious court of Richard II, which encouraged greater extravagance of dress and speedier changes in fashion."[12] Yet here, in Chaucer's portrait, is held up to them as ideal a man who "of fustian . . . wered a gypon / Al bismotered with his habergeon" (I, 75-76). *Actual* knights were attacked by the Church; Chaucer's Knight is in such a hurry to get on with his pilgrimage that he literally cannot pause for a change of linen. *Actual* knights were noted for "their arrogance, and their plundering activities"; Chaucer's is "of his port as meeke as is a mayde" (I, 69). And yet Chaucer's Knight is presented as being as palpably real as any actual plundering bully.

The Knight of the General Prologue is thus both ideal and real, though in a deeper sense than Lumiansky's contrast reveals him to be. He is idealized reality—an actual bismotered fighter just returned from a number of campaigns, yet tempered by a set of values presumably extinct in the chivalric class; and he is a realized ideal—a conventionalized, *Book-of-the-Duchess* piece of literary

perfection "al bismotered with his habergeon." Put the
two together, let the two concepts modify and define one
another, and the character, thus rounded, walks off the
page, a living paradox, "a verray, parfit gentil knyght"
(I, 72).

Chaucer's intention is clear in the paradox of that
masterful summarizing line: knights were ordinarily not
both "true" and "perfect." Yet this one is, and therein
lies the whole point of presenting a knight—and the other
characters as well—within the social context of a pilgrimage. Chaucer's audience, and we also, see the Knight
from three angles, in terms of three knights: the knight
of ideality, the knight of literary convention, and the
Knight of *The Canterbury Tales*, who is related to, though
not identifiable with, the other two.

Chaucer thus begins with the Knight in order to
introduce the reader to a character already known, in
actuality and in literature, in order to set, if not a pattern,
then a style, a means of seeing and knowing life. For, as
Ralph Baldwin and others have said, the great pilgrimage
to Canterbury is an image of life, of a journey "whose
destination becomes thereby neither Southwerk nor Canterbury, but the Holy City of Jerusalem."[13] Thus the
Host, that bumptious, thoroughly worldly and alive man,
full of impossible plans and judgments, must yield at the
end to the Parson, whom he has cursed and denied and
whose sermon is a general recapitulation of the sins of
the Canterbury pilgrims and thus of the whole world.

Seen in this fashion, the poem assumes a unity and
grandeur denied by critics who see it simply as a cleverly
organized anthology of medieval literature. The great
temptation, however, is to exaggerate Chaucer's intent in
framing such a unity. Following St. Paul and the Church
Fathers who glossed the scriptures, it has become usual
for modern critics who use patristic exegesis as a tool

of literary criticism to quote the doctrine of the Second
Epistle to Timothy that "all scripture is given by inspiration of God and is profitable for doctrine, for reproof,
for correction, for instruction in righteousness" and so
turn all medieval literature into didactic allegory.[14] That
allusion to scripture and the writings of the Church
Fathers underlies much of medieval literature and that
great portions of that literature were didactically conceived
scholars do not doubt. It is certain that patristical exegesis
has done much to illuminate poems such as *Piers Plowman* where the work is clearly written "for doctrine."[15]
But *The Canterbury Tales* is something else again, and
while the tone of the Retraction and of some of the later
tales, notably those of the Parson and the Second Nun,
would seem to indicate a didactic intent, we must
remember that the work as a whole (and in its various
parts) is dramatically and, I believe, descriptively conceived and that the Retraction, undeniably a late piece
of work, can no more be used to prove the intent of the
Knight's Tale, which it in effect renounces, than can *The
Tempest* be used to demonstrate Shakespeare's purpose in
writing *Love's Labours Lost*.

While I agree with Baldwin that *The Canterbury
Tales* recounts the journey not only from London to
Canterbury, but also from *Civitas Terrena* to the City of
God, and the pilgrims, "wayfarers in time, become *potius
mystice quam chronice*, wayfarers to eternity,"[16] I cannot
believe that Chaucer's intention is didactic except perhaps
as an afterthought in the Retraction, and that he, like
the Parson, set about "earnestly to construct an edifying
and corrective discourse."[17] While it is comparatively
easy to work backwards, as Baldwin does, through the
tales from the Retraction in demonstrating a didactic
intent, it is impossible to work forward in the tales in
attempting to prove that same purpose from any given

point in the pilgrimage, up to and including the Parson's own sermon. For one thing, the poem is everywhere dramatic and Chaucer the pilgrim is not necessarily Chaucer the writer *except in the Retraction*, where the tone and the startling lack of any dramatic context, even such as that supplied in the Introduction to the *Man of Law's Tale*, obviously reveal the writer's voice speaking. For all interpretive purposes, *The Canterbury Tales* ends with the *Parson's Tale*, even though Chaucer himself, at the end, may have thought otherwise.

Thus, I believe that while *The Canterbury Tales* was conceived by Chaucer originally as a "pilgrimage of the life of man,"[18] I do not think he intended it also to be a "rehearsal for death and the judgment."[19] The poem seems to me to be much more rationally viewed as an imitation of life, as a clear and loving description of the world, of the "way things are," as seen by a most clear-sighted yet most tolerant poet. *The Canterbury Tales* is an essay in observing and understanding, not in judging the world, and although any fair attempt at delineation of character or situation necessarily contains its own implicit evaluation and judgment, these need neither predetermine nor obscure the classical writer's initial intent simply to imitate what he sees in order to probe and understand its underlying form.

Chaucer has taken steps, moreover, to avoid any such misunderstandings of his motives. Whatever we may think about the characteristics and uses of the *persona* in medieval literature, Chaucer the pilgrim can best be understood as an active, articulate narrator deliberately conceived by the poet as a means of achieving aesthetic distance and of thus avoiding any imputation of value judgment by the reader directly to the author. The narrator frequently voices his reactions, either directly or by implication; we are never safe, except again perhaps in the Retraction, in ascribing those reactions to Chaucer the writer. I know (or at least I think I know) what Chaucer the pilgrim thought of the Sergeant of the Law; it would be extremely dangerous for me to guess what Chaucer the writer actually thought of Thomas Pynchbek.

The pilgrimage is thus an imitation of life in its movement from birth to death, from the Worldly City to the City of God, and if, at the end, the Host gives way to the Parson, this is a literary, if not perhaps an actual, inevitability. To return to one of my themes, the pilgrimage is a quest—though a quest of a different and more sophisticated nature than has appeared before. For this time the questor is not simply a knight, nor even, as a little later with Malory, a group of knights, but a whole society envisioned on a pilgrimage, "wayfarers in time, . . . wayfarers to eternity." As in the other poems, we are again thrown into contact with man's quest for self-knowledge, this time seen under the guise of *societas peregrina*, and again the pattern of the myth throws light upon the pattern of the poem.

It is important, however, that in *The Canterbury Tales* the quest is never completed, although Chaucer may have attempted to give the poem the semblance of a completed work.[20] There is little doubt, as there was, for example, with the romances of Chrétien, that Chaucer's poem possesses unity, dramatically in that tellers and tales are both parts of the pilgrimage "frame" which contains both and is the actual subject of the poem[21] and thematically in that both tellers and tales contribute to a whole view of life, "the actions of that feckless creature Man in his human comedy."[22] Despite the fact that *The Canterbury Tales* is a unified and perhaps also an almost-completed work, the myth which it reflects, that of the journey, is never properly concluded. Although we presume the pilgrimage at the end of *The Parson's Tale* to have reached Canterbury, we have no knowledge of its return to Southwerk, and in Toynbee's dictum the "return is the essence of the whole movement as well as its final cause."[23]

Chaucer never lived to complete *The Canterbury Tales* as it was originally planned;[24] hence we are left with a poem that never properly fulfills its pattern. We expect not only to be introduced to the characters but to see them develop as they come into contact with one another and, more importantly, with Canterbury. In Aristotle's terms, the poem lacks an "ending." This sense of incompleteness is, I expect, why on the one hand the theory that the poem is simply an anthology still finds a following in spite of the demonstrated unity of teller and tale with frame and why, on the other hand, *The Tale of Beryn*, the so-called *Second Merchant's Tale*, which relates the actions of the pilgrims in Canterbury, is so attractive. It is as though *Sir Gawain and the Green Knight* ended just as Gawain approached the Green Chapel. We miss the promised end and with it the sense of the whole and its final cause.

But society in *The Canterbury Tales* does set out to visit the *Civitas Dei* even though it never returns, and the theme of the poem as we have it must therefore be an imitation of life in its movement from birth to death, not of life as transformed by a visit, however brief and for whatever motives, to the New Jerusalem. Even so, the great theme of the pilgrimage is not the preparation for death but the nature of life. And the nature of living man, as Chaucer sees him, is to love.

The Canterbury Tales, from beginning to end, is an anatomy of love. It begins, as many critics have pointed out, in nature—"Whan that Aprill"—and in "the general Springtime surge of human energy and longing."[25] And the "two voices," as Arthur W. Hoffman calls them, of

love—the natural, profane love that impels and the supernatural, divine love that draws—call conjointly throughout
the General Prologue, in the relation of Knight and
Squire to each other and to their code, in the tension
between courtly and ecclesiastical values in the Prioress,
in the brotherhood of Parson and Plowman, the lechery
of the Friar, the vanity of the Monk, the austerity of the
Clerk, the Epicureanism of the Franklin, the greed of the
Physician, and the sensuality of the Wife of Bath.

Nor does the General Prologue suggest the almost
infinite number of changes that Chaucer rings upon his
theme in the work. Kittredge's marriage group,[26] for
example, sharply as it would seem to be defined, does
not nearly encompass Chaucer's discussion of marriage in
The Canterbury Tales. The various fabliaux, the *Man
of Law's Tale*, Chaucer's *Tale of Melibeus*, the *Nun's
Priest's Tale*, the *Second Nun's Tale*, the *Manciple's
Tale*, the Parson's sermon, the confessions of Harry Bailly
of his marital troubles—these also involve views of marriage. Enlarging the angle of focus to include all manner
of love between the sexes, all of the tales except perhaps
those of the Friar, Summoner, and Canon's Yeoman are
involved, each tale adding its bit of observation. "And
yet," says the Man of Law to the Miller, and the Merchant replies, "But still."

It is this movement of ideas, opinions, and observa-
tions backward and forward among the pilgrims, not only
outwardly in the links, but covertly in the chiming and
echoing of sentiment and image in the tales, that is the
real subject of the book, Chaucer's imitation of the living
world of his own time. The Prioress slyly—"or elles [as
monks] oghte be" (VII, 643)—rebukes the Monk; the
Nun's Priest's self-righteous, intellectual hen in turn
rebukes the Prioress. The Prioress warmly sentimentalizes
almost beyond recognition her tale of the martyred "litel

clergeon"; the Second Nun in her fanatical life of St. Cecilia corrects the impression of nuns given by her superior. Among the pilgrims, in the links and within the tales, the conversation goes on, and the enduring subject is love.

Nor are paternal, filial, and divine love neglected. Fraternal and filial love and their relation to sexuality form the bases of the Knight's and Physician's tales. The love of God for man and man for God plays a major role in the tales of the Second Nun, the Monk, and the Prioress. And loyalty—of comrade to comrade, of subject to lord—which is a kind of love, the obverse of trickery and deceit, can be seen to underlie all the tales, even the fabliaux.

This is a long preamble to a discussion of Chaucer's Knight, but it is this theme, this involved analysis of the uses of love in society, that Chaucer introduces by means of the Knight both in the General Prologue—"And at a knyght than wol I first bigynne"—and in the tales—"the cut fil to the Knyght" (I, 845).

One often hears that in Chaucer's portrayal of the Knight he extolled his ideal of knighthood and that in the *Rime of Sir Thopas* he satirized the degenerate reality.[27] Though oversimplified, this idea reflects an interesting critical point of view. For certainly the portraits of the Knight and Squire in the General Prologue, the *Knight's Tale*, the *Squire's Tale*, and the *Rime of Sir Thopas* are meant by Chaucer to be read within a single context, that of the Canterbury pilgrimage, and thus all influence the composite image of the knight presented in the poem. Nor can we really stop with these obvious pieces. The *Wife of Bath's Tale*, the *Franklin's Tale*, and, to a lesser degree, the tales of the Merchant and Clerk also involve knights and chivalric love.

The *Knight's Tale* both begins the storytelling game

and reinforces the picture of the Knight presented in the General Prologue. The most coherent view of the suiting of the *Knight's Tale* to the personality of its teller is that of R. M. Lumiansky,[28] who demonstrates how Chaucer has rewritten Boccaccio's *Teseide* for the Knight to enable a standard chivalric romance to bear a heavy cargo of Boethian philosophy appropriate to a knight whose bearing and demeanor in the General Prologue suggest a philosophical turn of mind.

The Boethian element in the *Knight's Tale* introduces the reader, moreover, to the same kaleidoscopic vision of love exhibited throughout in the General Prologue. For the Knight's interest in Boethius does not lie simply in the questions of free will and predestination, chance and heavenly purpose, that form the core of the *De Consolatione,* but more specifically in the relation of those issues to chivalric love. The changes of fortune and attitude through which Palamon and Arcite pass are determined not by Dame Fortuna alone, as Lumiansky's analysis of the influence of fortune upon the action indicates, but also by Fortuna's delivering the young men into the snares of *fin amor.* The reason for the conflict between the young men and hence their cause for questioning the workings of the universe is their falling in love at first sight, a usual part of the courtly love ritual. Granted that the main actions of the cousins are initiated by "cas" or "aventure" or "nature," these accidents would have had no effect upon them if the young men were not so deeply involved in courtly love. Thus, Arcite's refusal to accept his *good* "fortune" in being released from prison and his insistence of returning to Athens in spite of Theseus's commands are caused not so much by the god Mercury's summons (which Chaucer hints [I, 1374 ff.] may be a hallucination) as by the facts that the malady of love had driven him nearly mad and that this disease had so altered his appearance that he could easily escape detection in Athens. Much the same sort of thing may be said for the other actions of Arcite and Palamon; they may be propelled on their way to self-knowledge by a Boethian Fortuna, but their actions are guided primarily by the dictates of *fin amor*, which run opposed to those of reason in the poem.

The two great summarizing thematic speeches in the *Knight's Tale*, however, belong not to the young men but to Theseus. His first pronouncement, made upon discovering the exiled Arcite and the escaped Palamon fighting over Emily rather than attempting to escape his judgment, is thoroughly in the spirit of much of *Troilus and Criseyde*[29] and relates the Boethian theme of free will and predestination to courtly love by arguing that the God of Love is stronger than any of the other influences governing man's conduct. Who except Love could place these men in jeopardy of their lives and reward their devotion only with wounds: "Now looketh, is nat that an heigh folye? / Who may been a fool, but if he love" (I, 1798-99)? The point of Theseus's speech is very exact; if "cas" has influenced the actions of the young men, then it has done so as an agent of Love, for Love has "maugree hir eyen two, / Broght hem hyder bothe for to dye" (I, 1796-97).

Theseus's final speech celebrating the great chain of love which unites all things again brings together the themes of fortune and love. Both must at the last be judged unaccountable, unknowable, unpredictable, at least in earthly terms, and wise men would do well to "maken virtu of necessitee, / And take it weel that we may nat eschue" (I, 3042-43), a thoroughly Boethian conclusion to the whole problem.

And a significant beginning to the storytelling game. The great theme, love, has been introduced, not as a

settled doctrine or even as a remedy but as a practical
philosophic problem. What, asks the Knight, has love
done for these two men? True, one of the Jacks has
found a Jill, but the other, equally virtuous and deserving,
lies "in his colde grave / Allone, withouten any com-
paignye" (I, 2778-79). Both have endured hardship and
torment for the sake of love. Both have been exposed
nakedly to all the slings and arrows of outrageous Fortuna
with no protection from the shields of will and purpose.
And the Knight, for all his experience and study, can
make no more of it than to declare that we had best make
a virtue of necessity. It is a pregnant beginning to the
drama, and it reveals here at the end of the chivalric
tradition a new kind of hero, the questioning, searching,
philosophical knight, who in the fifteenth century appears
briefly as Malory's Bors and who two hundred years after
Chaucer speaks from behind Spenser's allegorical masks
and from the mouth of Shakespeare's King Harry.

The tales of the Wife of Bath and Franklin reveal also
within their own dramatic contexts something about the
philosophical knight. The *Wife of Bath's Tale* is the story
of the conversion of a young arrogant aristocrat to the
ways of true *gentilesse*. A rapist, this "lusty bacheler"
accepts blithely the help of the loathly lady only to
resist violently and in the ugliest, most insulting terms
her proposal of marriage—"My love?" quod he, "nay, my
dampnacioun!" (III, 1067). However, the hag's bed-
curtain speech on the nature of true *gentilesse*, which
stems neither from youth nor wealth nor family but from
the gentle heart, shames the knight into an admission
of his own unworthiness and inability to govern himself.[30]
In the act of relinquishing to his wife his right of decision,
he gains not only a beautiful and faithful wife, but also,
at least in the eyes of Dame Alison, wisdom.

If we void our minds for a moment of the Wife's immediate purpose in telling her tale—her doctrinaire preaching of female sovereignty—and of her pathetic, unconscious identification of herself with the transformed hag, we can see the outlines of the pilgrim-Knight. Here is the historical reality in the process of becoming the ideal of the General Prologue; transformed by an understanding of the nature of *gentilesse*, bully here yields before our eyes to philosopher.

The *Franklin's Tale* reveals much the same process, though here the immediate catalyst is not the generalized *gentilesse*, but love as a part of courtly life. It is evident that the essential conflict of the tale, the dilemma in which the Lady Dorigen finds herself, stems from the attempt of her husband and herself to carry with them into the sacramental bonds of marriage, in which the husband is lord and master of his wife, the practices of courtly love, which insists on the sovereignty of the lady.[31] This arrangement, as could be expected, almost results in tragedy, since Arveragus must, according to the knightly code, go a-tourneying and Dorigen must play the part of the courtly lady, accepting against her better judgment the attentions of a courtly lover. Dorigen's salvation is her decision to accept her rightful place as a dutiful wife: she tells Arveragus of her difficulty, and although he at first (V, 1467) in courtly fashion takes her problem lightly, he soon, like Dorigen, understands the importance of their misjudgment of marriage. Thus, though he must insist upon Dorigen's fulfilling her promise, since fidelity to one's word is a necessity in both courtship and marriage, he does so with a heavy heart (V, 1480).

It seems to me that this tale, like the Wife of Bath's, revolves about the hero's realization (and here also the heroine's) of the essential dishonesty of the chivalric code. The *Wife of Bath's Tale* condemns the superficial values of youth, birth, and wealth and praises the true *gentilesse* of the spirit. The *Franklin's Tale* exposes the immorality inherent in courtly values and praises the bourgeois ideal of marriage. While both tales avoid tragedy only by the intervention—significantly, I think—of a *deus ex machina*, their happy endings result from the conversion of their heroes from a false chivalry to a more practical, though nonetheless idealistic, set of values.

These tales clarify considerably the composite portrait of the knight of the *Canterbury Tales*. The philosophical Knight's query into the nature of courtly love, whether it indeed brings anything but sorrow in the form of adverse "cas" and "aventure," is answered by the chivalric romances of the Wife of Bath and the Franklin, in which knightly heroes, by rejecting the conventionalized immorality of Andreas Capellanus, admitting their error, and accepting reason, actually bring *good* "aventure" and "cas" upon themselves in the form of the *dei ex machina*.

It is no wonder that the pointless romance begun by the Squire, who, in spite of his obvious attractiveness, lacks his father's depth and wisdom, is abandoned by Chaucer as having no real place in his presentation of chivalric values and that Chaucer himself tells a burlesque of the extravagances, though not of the ideals, of chivalry. For Chaucer is no longer content to write according to the conventions of romance; the knight as Chaucer portrays him within the context of the Canterbury pilgrimage bears almost no resemblance to the Black Knight of *The Book of the Duchess*. He is now older, and with age have come not only experience and wisdom, but also a dissatisfaction with the poses and mannerisms of chivalry, though not with its ideals. The knight has come to love philosophy, and his philosophy has led him to the bourgeois ideals of marriage and natural *gentilesse*, concepts alien to traditional chivalry. In his Knight, Chaucer has defined a new concept of chivalry for a new age, a chivalry stripped of its immorality and criminal violence and ready to stand in the midst of the new mercantilism as a symbol of the conservative values that Chaucer everywhere praises.

THE TRAGIC KNIGHT

MALORY'S *MORTE DARTHUR*

A LTHOUGH the code of chivalry had by the late fifteenth century ceased to have any military or political importance in England and although knighthood had become a faintly archaic social institution, to the writer of the age chivalry was not yet wholly a lost cause, the "fragrance of an irretrievable past."[1] The popular writers of the fifteenth century—Stephen Hawes, Stephen Scrope, Sir Gilbert Hay, and, of course, Malory and Caxton—wrote or translated many books, tracts, and pamphlets concerning knightly warfare and behavior, books which while they reflect more accurately the desires of the Tudor family to "romanticize its British origins"[2] than to teach actual conduct, nevertheless attest to the popularity of courtly literature even a hundred years after the death of Chaucer.

Thus although the preceding century had witnessed both the demise of chivalry as an active military code and the beginning of its transformation into a political ideal,[3] it had not forgotten the tradition of the military knight errant and his role. The author of *Piers Plowman*, for example, promotes an ideal of knighthood as the agency of the crown for defense of the realm and the "comune" (C, xviii, 289-91). Although the "military function of the knight" had long since begun to give way to "his civil duties as a governor,"[4] the author of *Piers Plowman* still thought of the knight, as I expect did nearly all the "comune," "in its military, chivalric sense, without political connotation."[5]

Thus in spite of the historical changes in the character and function of the knight "from medieval knight into . . . Tudor governor,"[6] the popular ideal, the "image," of the knight did not change. In an age of violent and upsetting transition like the fifteenth century, when men were being forced by uncontrollable events out of the feudal and Catholic way of life and into Renaissance and Reformation, the literary portrait of chivalry must have seemed to aristocrats like Malory to embody the stability in standards which England most needed. The humiliating defeats in France and the chaos of the Wars of the Roses at home became the cause both of the "chivalric revival" of the fifteenth century, with its self-conscious and slightly decadent rituals, and of its reemphasizing in works such as Caxton's translation of *The Boke of the Ordre of Chyvalry* the history of monarchs like Edward III and Henry V and hence the ideals to which living knights should attain as inheritors of that great tradition:

Oh ye knights of England, where is the custom and usage of noble chivalry that was used in those days? What do ye now but go to the bagnios and play at dice? And some not well advised use not honest and good rule against all order of knighthood. Leave this, leave it and read the noble volumes of the Holy Grail, of Launcelot, of Galahad, of Tristram, of Perseforest, of Percival, of Gawain, and many more. And look in later days of the noble acts since the conquest, as in the days of King Richard, Coeur de Lyon, Edward the First and

Third and his noble sons. . . . Read Froissart. And also
behold that victorious and noble king, Harry the Fifth, and
the captains under him. . . .[7]

Thus, it is a mistake to view Malory's *Morte Darthur*
simply as a sentimental excursion into a long-dead past.
To a degree, it is this, but it is much more. It is also a
didactic work, a plea to the fifteenth-century English
knights to learn a lesson from the past, to see in the
internal struggle for power in Arthur's court a meaningful
parallel to their own civil conflicts and to avoid the
pitfalls of history by reasserting the simple code of conduct
implicit in the high ideals of legendary chivalry: ". . .
never to do outerage nothir morthir, and allwayes to fle
treson, and to gyff mercy unto hym that askith mercy,
uppon payne of forfiture [of their] worship and lordship
of kynge Arthure for evirmore; and allwayes to do ladyes,
damesels, and jantilwomen and wydowes [socour:] strenghe
hem in hir ryghtes, and never to enforce them, uppon
payne of dethe."[8]

But the *Morte Darthur* is also a great literary tragedy.
Observed apart from its relation to its age and seen in
the light of its literary tradition, Malory's book reflects,
below and running counter to its historical, didactic surface, a deeply tragic awareness of chivalry's failure to
attain perfection. It is to a degree true that Malory would
have preferred it otherwise and that Vinaver and Ferguson
are right in asserting that Malory at times made an effort
to remove from the book those attributes of the chivalric
code—courtly love, religious mysticism, the "gently cynical
realism"[9] of Sir Dinadan—of which he personally disap-
proved and which he did not wish included in the code
of behavior that he envisioned as proper for his kind of
knight, the Tory military agrarian of the fifteenth century.
But despite his strict notions of chivalric propriety and

his provincial English prejudices,[10] Malory was in the end powerless to change the essential elements of the Arthurian legend. From the beginning, the book is larger than the man and the artist stronger than the reformer. Malory's conscious desire to bring some sort of unity to the chaotically framed legend and to arrange the loosely bound episodes of his sources into a coherent structure transcends whatever simple, didactic message he may have had. Where artistry and the desire for reform conflict, as they occasionally do in the book, Malory prefers a consistent tragic book to an ill-formed moral one.

Such a view differs from the more traditional views about chivalry in the *Morte Darthur*. As I understand it, the usual line taken by literary and cultural historians— Vinaver, Ferguson, and P. E. Tucker, for example—maintains that Malory strongly advocated a practical and ethical chivalry far removed from the courtly code found in his sources, whose main purpose had been "to serve as an expression of the thoughts and emotions inspired by courtly idealism, to translate in terms of actions and characters the subtle varieties of courtly sentiment and the highly sophisticated code of courtly behavior."[11] Critics argue that Malory removed from his sources all praise of elements, such as courtly love or Cistercian mysticism or the cynicism of Dinadan,[12] that he thought debilitating to knighthood as he conceived of it and that he, to point a moral for his own time, blamed the tragedy of the Round Table on a "conflict of two loyalties, both deeply rooted in the medieval conception of knightly service: on the one hand, the heroic loyalty of man to man . . . ; on the other, the blind devotion of the knight-lover to his lady. . . ."[13] Thus it is said that Malory suddenly became aware of his hero Lancelot's inherent sinfulness halfway through the book[14] and that while he "does not condone the sin of Lancelot," Lancelot remains for him the "best of 'earthly sinful' men and his hero—a tragic hero, but one in whom the good greatly outweighted the bad."[15]

While I have possibly blurred the edges of the ethical, didactical approach to Malory by presenting in a composite the views of several critics, I hope I have nevertheless struck its central note—the essential practicality of Malory's approach to chivalry; "it is the chivalry strictly of an agrarian and military caste, and interpreted as far as possible in terms of realism and common sense."[16] Yet tempting as this view is, it contains an apparently insuperable paradox: how could a writer who set out certainly to praise and perhaps even to revive a dying chivalry have concluded by so effectively damning it; the chivalric ideal, as interpreted by Malory's hero, Lancelot, is shown to be in itself open to attacks of immorality, corruption, fraud, and treason and singularly ineffective in warding off the ravages of these attacks. Vinaver and Tucker resolve this difficulty by affirming, on slim evidence, that Malory's concept and understanding of the story evolved as he wrote it, that he discovered these discordant elements in his sources as he progressed and developed a *sens* to fit this new *matière*. But such a theory does not explain adequately either the dour prophecies of the early books or the evidence that Malory had acquired considerable knowledge of his sources before he began his own work.[17]

I submit, on the principle of Occam's Razor, that it is easier to abandon this self-contradictory "didactic" view of the *Morte Darthur* and to substitute for it a genuinely "tragic" view of a unified *Morte* than to attempt to reconcile the "didactic" interpretation with Malory's text. Nor is there any great danger in advancing such an insistently literary approach to the book of "losing sight of Malory himself and, more particularly, of the larger characteristics of his thinking."[18] For on our answer to the "literary" question of whether or not Malory did indeed wish to unify his work depends, initially, our view of Malory's intention in writing the book and, ultimately, our judgment of whether he was a rather simple-minded social reformer or a gifted writer whose tragic view of life moved him to recreate in one sustained narrative the passage of a civilization from beginning to end, from its hopeful and innocent youth to its tragic decay and destruction.

I believe that Malory attempted the latter, that his book reveals a single great theme—the rise, flowering, decay, and fall of a well-nigh perfect earthly civilization —and that to communicate this theme he drew three clear narrative lines from the tangled mazes of undirected incident that made up his immediate sources: the feud of the houses of Lot and Pellinore, the Grail quest, and the adultery of Lancelot and Guinevere. All of these involved the same characters and chronology and so became for Malory a scheme to give unity and focus to the legend. In any consideration of the *Morte Darthur* it is thus important to consider the nature of these three strong narrative cables since they determine the tone of the work by controlling and giving focus to Malory's structural design.

Taken separately, the three narratives are superficially unlike; a tale of a family blood feud, a semi-mystical religious tract, and a romance of lovers' intrigue would not seem to be suited for inclusion in the same library, much less the same work. Yet despite these obvious differences in subject—and we should remember that these differences account for the immense variety of incident and character in the *Morte Darthur*—Malory's three strains have at least two important characteristics, as well as characters, in common. First, each of the three deals with one of the essential aspects of chivalric knighthood—loyalty, piety, and love—qualities which mark the three decisive stages in the development of the historical knight: the feudal vassal, the crusading soldier, and the courtly lover. This is a fact of the greatest importance, I think, to anyone studying the *Morte Darthur*. For I am convinced that Malory's decision to unify the structure of his book through a concentration on these particular narrative strains was based neither on the arrangement of his sources nor on chance but on the discovery that each of these narrative lines expressed one vital aspect of his overall theme, each contributed its part to the definition of the chivalric life with which the book is centrally concerned. By means of Malory's structural revisions, we are permitted to see the face of the knight in each of his traditional historical and literary roles—as soldier, as Christian, and as lover.

The second quality which these three plot lines share qualifies the first. Each of the three plots of the book begins in a happy dawn of naive innocence and hope but ends in dissolution, decay, and tragedy. The quarrel between the families of King Lot and King Pellinore begins as a simple family quarrel but in time involves the whole court and splits the Round Table into a Gawain faction and a Lancelot faction. The Grail quest begins in rapture and vision but, as the King foresees, debilitates the strength of the Round Table and destroys the unity of the kingdom. Our first view of Lancelot the lover is of a rather grave, idealistic young man sending as trophies to the Queen those knights he has overcome, completely unaware of the effect that his later attachment to Guinevere will have on the court.

The central theme which these narrative lines emphasize is not simply the nature of chivalry, but more exactly the *tragic* nature of the Round Table civilization and, hence, of the courtly life. There would be little point in attempting to establish precisely what definitions of tragedy can be linked historically and externally to Malory and the *Morte Darthur*. Malory most likely thought of tragedy, if he ever attempted a definition, in the usual medieval terms of the arbitrary wheel spinning of Dame Fortune, whose dictates caused even the most deserving heroes to be cast down by sheer chance.

But even among the pagans who invented it the image and doctrine of Fortune's wheel was at best a makeshift attempt to explain the irrational play of chance in life. Although Boethius and the Fathers converted the pagan belief in chance to Christian use by assigning to Fortuna the role of God's unwitting handmaiden, the doctrine continued to be more descriptive than explanatory and, because it did not adequately explain the human predicament, never really became a satisfactory basis for tragedy. Chaucer's Monk, for example, having explained carefully the theory that all men are fated to fall from high to low estate "whan that Fortune list to flee," proceeds in his seventeen instances of the untrustworthy nature of the false felicity of earthly glory to describe what are actually seventeen examples of how pride of place or of intellect, sheer foolhardy *hubris*, leads to a fall. Lucifer, the Monk tells us, fell "for his synne," Adam for "mysgoveraunce," Samson for "wommen," and so on through the list. The tragedy of Grettir in the *Grettis saga*, though attributed by everyone in the book to his "luck," actually results from *hubris*, from his insistence on matching his unusual, though merely human strength with that of the ghost of Glam, who curses his presumption. To come forward a bit in time, despite Shakespeare's proclamation that Romeo and Juliet are "star-crossed lovers," their tragedy can be attributed more directly to Romeo's cocky rashness than to fate. In short, medieval tragedy, no matter how explained, actually demonstrated that false felicity led directly to spiritual blindness and that the resultant *hubris*, not the initial "luck," was the real cause of the hero's downfall.

Despite the single appearance of the wheel of Fortune in the *Morte Darthur* (1233),[19] the strongly articulated element of Fate in Book I and Malory's own beliefs, whatever they may have been, about the nature of tragedy, we cannot dismiss the *Morte Darthur* as simply a tragedy of fate. I have attempted elsewhere to define the tragedy of the fall of Arthur's court in Aristotelian terms, as a self-ordained tragedy precipitated by the *hamartiai* of the court—by Lancelot's instability, Arthur's dogged blindness, the queen's lechery, Gawain's unreasoning temper. Although the Aristotelian dicta can help to explain much of the *Morte Darthur*, there still is much about the book it does not explain, principally its conclusion. For it is the essence of Aristotelian tragedy that it end in a kind of moral victory in which the base emotions of pity and fear, having been aroused by the initial action, are purged. Lear, stripped of kingship and power, reaches in his poverty and degradation a nobility of spirit far surpassing his former temporal majesty. Oedipus, once blinded by pride, comes to understand himself as he truly is, and having resisted in *Oedipus at Colonnus* all the temptations he had once been prey to, is assumed into the company of gods.

The *Morte Darthur* fails precisely here. The heroes fall, but they fall in ignorance, and the "dolorous death and departing" of the great court is accompanied by no upsurge of spirit and by no illumination of self. Guinevere takes the veil and Lancelot dies in orders, but these are the expedients of the times; and their final interview is filled only with regrets for the past, not with the vision of a new life:

And they departed; but there was never so harde an herted man but he wold have wepte to see the dolour that they made, for there was lamentacyon as they had be stungyn wyth sperys, and many tymes they swouned. And the ladyes bare the quene to hir chambre.

And syr Launcelot awok, and went and took hys hors, and rode al that day and al nyght in a forest wepyng. (1253-54)

Gawain's dying letter to Lancelot is filled with remorse that he "soughte [Lancelot's] dethe, and nat thorow [Lancelot's] deservynge, but [his] owne sekynge" (1231). Ector's great eulogy looks backward to the youthful triumphs of Lancelot and praises only those qualities which destroyed him—his prowess, his love for the Queen, his chivalry. We are not convinced that his last holy days brought him either peace or self-knowledge, only a "broken slepe" in which he saw himself "lyeing grovelyng on the tombe of kyng Arthur and quene Guenever, and there was no comforte that the Bysshop, nor syr Bors, nor none of his felowes coude make hym, it avaylled not" (1257). Arthur, whose vision and energy and whose sins had framed the new chivalry, dies disillusioned and haunted by failure. "Comforte thyselff, . . . and do as well as thou mayste, for in me ys no truste for to truste in," (1240) he says at the last to Bedivere, and though in Tennyson he goes on to prophesy a new and better world, in Malory he sees only the total destruction of his own order.

No one in the *Morte Darthur*, except Bors, really comes to know himself, and therein lies a tragedy deeper than that defined by Aristotle. The folly of the court, predicted by Merlin and foreshadowed in Balin, persists to the end. Granted that the chivalric code is shot through with contradictions—that knights must swear to respect and protect women in a society which regularly indulges in the practices of courtly love, that they go off to search for the Grail armed as if for battle, that they plot against a king to whom they yearly pledge fealty. But they fail always to rise above the code, to examine it and themselves in the light of its failures, and so they perish clutching to a way of life, to a system they can no longer bend to meet their needs and that has failed to provide its promised ends. In modern philosophical terms the knights have placed "essences," theoretical standards of behavior, before the facts of "existence." The Grail quest, though in the spirit of chivalry's view of itself, was from its hasty inception an impossible presumption for everyone except the Grail knights; the intrigue of Lancelot and Guinevere, though conducted according to the rules of *fin amor*, could not continue unnoticed and without consequence; the brutal feud of the houses of Lot and Pellinore, though proceeding from the most respected motives, was certain to erupt eventually into civil war. As with Milton's Eve, at whom every reader wants to scream, "Look, woman; can't you see that's a *snake*," we see what the knights cannot, the folly of the code to which they adhere. Only Bors, who rejects chivalric standards, refusing to take up arms even to defend his brother, achieves self-knowledge and so becomes Lancelot's most trusted, though ironically his most unheeded, advisor.

In the end the failure of the knights lies not so much in their code as in their failure to examine themselves and their society and to transcend the destruction of Arthur's kingdom. Unlike Oedipus and unlike even Hamlet who is trapped in the meshes of his perpetual self-examination, the knights go bitterly to their deaths, relentlessly whoring after strange gods.

One cannot say to what degree this tragic concept of knighthood is Malory's own and how much is inherent in the legend as he received it from his sources. That the tragic fall of the court is implicit in all forms of the story from Geoffrey of Monmouth onwards is obvious, though it is largely ignored in most of the early French romances. But though the final events are dutifully recorded in Malory's sources for these last books, the English stanzaic Le Morte Arthure and the Vulgate Mort Artu, they are never given the precise emphasis that Malory gives them, chiefly through the reactions of the knights and ladies to the tragedy confronting them. As Vinaver concludes, having analyzed those passages in these final pages that have no source, "having transferred the tragedy of Arthurian knighthood to [an] essentially human plane, Malory could only make it convincing by emphasizing those emotions which, in his conception, had brought it about—the passionate feudal loyalty of man to man [seen in the Lot-Pellinore feud] and the self-denying devotion of the knight-lover to his lady [seen in the Lancelot-Guinevere intrigue]"[20] to which I should add the devotion of the court to an unattainable religious ideal, the Grail quest. Thus Malory adds Gawain's letter, Arthur's final bitter statement that "truste" is gone, Ector's lament—those passages that define the "essentially human plane" on which he is working and so best illustrate the human blindness and tragedy, unrelieved by any sort of spiritual triumph, that mark the ending of the Morte Darthur.

I realize that I have emerged with an "existential Malory," and it might be argued that I am reading a great deal into Malory by assigning to him a theory of tragedy he could not possibly have held. But I do not believe that I am misreading the Morte Darthur. For the book does end in despair and with the burial of the chivalric ideal. Malory, by the didactic view of the book, may very well be warning his contemporaries against the excesses of chivalry; he may even, as Caxton thought, be lamenting the tragedy of its fall; but he is not in the "hoole book" either defending or attempting to revive chivalry as a panacea for his own troubled times. In Malory, the knight perishes by his own hand, to be revived briefly, though only as a shadow, in Spenser's allegorical figures and to become finally in Sir Toby Belch and Sir Andrew Aguecheek the property of groundlings.

From Roland to Lancelot is a long journey indeed, but in spite of the many bypaths, the down-sloping road between them may be mapped with fair accuracy. As the knight, like the court he represents, becomes more sophisticated, he becomes more complex, more a creature of the fallen world of mixed good and evil. Roland is in a sense the Adam of knighthood; his primitive simplicity and innocence are the signs of a virtue uncomplicated by mixed motives and values. "Pagans are wrong and Christians are right," says the author of *La Chanson de Roland*, and the reader is expected to approve that statement without reservation.

Lancelot stands at the opposite pole; every statement of his greatness must be hedged round with qualifications:

'Sir, I say you sothe,' seyde the damesell, 'for ye were thys day in the morne the best knyght of the worlde. But who sholde sey so now, he sholde be a lyer, for there ys now one bettir than ye be, and well hit ys preved by the adventure of the swerde whereto ye durst nat sette to your honde. And that ys the change of youre name and levynge. Wherefore I make unto you a remembraunce that ye shall not wene frome hensforthe that ye be the best knyght of the worlde.' (863)

Even Sir Ector's funeral lament reveals by implication Lancelot's imperfections by calling him "the trewest lover of a synful man that ever loved woman" (1259).

It will be helpful, I think, to examine Malory's book

in relation to the myth of knighthood, the quest of the hero from ignorance to self-knowledge, the *rite de passage* from childhood, at whatever age, to full, knowing manhood. Such a process was comparatively easy in *Erec et Enide* and in *Sir Gawain and the Green Knight*, since these romances, however complex their plots, dealt with the adventures of a single knight. The *Morte Darthur* is full of knights and quests, so we are immediately faced as in *The Canterbury Tales* with the prospect of dealing in mythical terms with society as hero. Viewed in this way, the whole Arthurian court becomes the protagonist of Malory's book and the "rise, flowering, decay, and fall of a well-nigh perfect earthly civilization" its quest.

More particularly, however, it is the quest for the Holy Grail that epitomizes, though it does not necessarily cause, the failure of the Arthurian dream. Here, significantly, is the one quest in which the whole court participates; here is the quest most alien by its nature to the usual tasks and successes of the Arthurian knight; here is the quest most surrounded from its inception by a sense of foreboding and tragedy: " 'Now,' seyde the kynge, 'I am sure at this quest of the Sankegreall shall all ye of the Rownde Table departe, and nevyr shall I se you agayne hole togydir, therefore ones shall I se you togydir in the medow, all hole togydirs!' " And Arthur rebukes Gawain, who rashly instituted the quest: " 'A, Gawayne, Gawayne! Ye have betrayed me, for never shall my courte be amended by you.' "

The Grail quest is also the quest closest in pattern to the hero myth. Its challenge comes suddenly upon the court and will not be refused; it demands of the knights complete abandonment of their normal activities and forces them to cross over into a strange land marked by terrors and dangers; and it offers to Arthur's society the ultimate gift from God, the guardianship of the Grail, the creation on earth of the *Civitas Dei*, in C. S. Lewis's phrase, the unification of "Christianity and civilization."[21]

The Grail quest, like the quest of the Round Table for perfection, is a failure, and the myth pattern is never completed. True, the knights receive and accept the challenge and some even cross the frontiers of the alien land, but once there the great quest dissipates into aimless, frustrated wanderings. To recall from our discussion of Chrétien the terms of Joseph Campbell, we see this time a quest destroyed by its failure to secure its ultimate boon, the Holy Grail, the elixir of life, a "grace capable of both energizing and giving meaning"[22] to a civilization well on its way to destruction. It is significant that Lancelot, the greatest exemplar of chivalry, though he sees the Grail cannot attain it and that although three of the knights, Galahad, Perceval, and Bors, do attain the Grail, the lifegiving relic is not returned to Arthur's court but taken by Galahad to the mystical land of Sarras.

Stated another way, Malory sees the whole myth of the hero, and not just the particular mores of chivalry or of the Arthurian court, in tragic terms. Northrop Frye, in a penetrating analysis of the forms that the quest myth, which he like Joseph Campbell regards as the "single pattern of significance" and the "central myth of literature,"[23] may take, delineates four "phases" or shapes of the myth corresponding roughly to the four seasons of the year. These phases may be correlated with the various forms of the hero myth discussed by Campbell and, more importantly, can be seen to correspond to the actual forms of chivalric literature. Most of the courtly romances certainly reflect the "dawn, spring, and birth phase" of the myth with their emphasis on the "birth of the hero, . . . revival and resurrection, . . . creation and the defeat of the powers of darkness, winter, and death."[24] Seen in terms of Frye's analysis, the myth of the hero as it appears in the *Morte Darthur*, however, is in its "sunset, autumn, and death phase," which is marked by "myths of fall, of the dying god [Arthur? Lancelot?], of violent death and sacrifice [Gareth?] and of the isolation of the hero [Lancelot's exile?]." Its "subordinate characters" are "the traitor [Mordred] and the siren [Morgause? Guinevere?]," and it is "the archetype of tragedy and elegy."

I do not mean to suggest that either of these overly systematic approaches to myth in literature be applied in detail to the *Morte Darthur*; needless to say, Malory was blissfully unconscious of the new mythography. Yet because both Campbell and Frye deal with universals, their patterns are relevant to the literature of the chivalric tradition and to Malory. Erec and Yvain, though they are temporarily detained, complete their quests and reach the "zenith, summer, and marriage" phase of the myth, which is marked by "sacred marriage" and "entering into Paradise" and which has as its principal subordinate characters the "companion and the bride." The quest of Lancelot in Chrétien's portion of *The Knight of the Cart* is, on the other hand, never completed and that of Gawain for the Green Knight, while completed, is rendered useless by the failure of Arthur's court to accept the values for which the quest was made. In Frye's terms, *Sir Gawain and the Green Knight* is a "winter" phase of the myth marked by the defeat of the hero, inhabited, interestingly enough, by "ogres and witches," and reflecting the "archetype of satire." Chaucer's Knight is not himself a questor, and the pilgrimage, the quest on which he rides, ends prematurely. Yet the knights of Chaucer's tales, like Chrétien's knights, attain transforming wisdom which elevates both them and the concept of knighthood.

All this is conjectural, but it is to the point, for no matter what terms one uses, it makes considerable sense

to say that from Roland to Lancelot we have moved from
success to failure, from heroic comedy to tragedy, and
that Chrétien, the Gawain poet, and Chaucer profess
attitudes somewhere between the two extremes. Yvain
and Erec learn through suffering, making their knighthood
both meaningful and worthwhile; Gawain in the English
romance recognizes the tragic dualism of knighthood, but
cannot communicate it to the court; Chaucer's knights
transform the basis of knighthood by turning pride into
humility and so adjust themselves to a new age and
society.

But Malory's Lancelot can do none of these things,
and so his tragedy and that of the court become for the
first time in literature tragic as well as inevitable:

My synne and my wyckednes hath brought me unto grete
dishonoure! For whan I sought worldly adventures for worldely
desyres I ever encheved them and had the bettir in every
place, and never was I discomfite in no quarell, were hit
ryght were hit wronge. And now I take uppon me the
adventures to seke of holy thynges, now I se and undirstonde
that myne olde synne hyndryth me and shamyth me, that I
had no power to stirre nother speke whan the holy bloode
appered before me. (896)

At the end of the Grail quest, Galahad bids Bors, who
unlike Lancelot has renounced chivalry to achieve salvation, to "salew me unto my lorde sir Launcelot, my fadir,
and as sone as ye se hym bydde hym remembir of this
worlde unstable" (1035). It is the tragedy of Lancelot,
and of the chivalry of the Round Table, that they are
forever committed to "this worlde unstable."

THE ALLEGORICAL KNIGHT

THE FAERIE QUEENE

EDMUND Spenser wrote *The Faerie Queene* during the waning years of the Tudor revival of the rites of chivalry and of a nationalized Arthurian legend. Since the time of Geoffrey of Monmouth in the twelfth century, the widely circulated stories of King Arthur and the Round Table both had furnished patriotic Englishmen with an idealized picture of knighthood which, as we have seen, had no factual basis and had symbolized to them their national heritage of honor and gallantry. Geoffrey's *Historia Regum Britanniae*, which first documented what was almost certainly an already flourishing tradition of Arthur's chivalric miracles, itself probably was motivated not only by Geoffrey's desire to present a historic picture of the chivalric past but also by his intention to establish less than a hundred years after the Norman invasion the image of a native British hero fit to counter France's Charlemagne. Certainly from the time of Geoffrey onward, to the Englishman "Arthur" and "chivalry" were nearly synonymous terms.

In a sense the Arthurian legend in its long development reflects like a radar screen the fortunes of chivalry in England. In Geoffrey and Layamon, Arthur is a king of battles, a bushy, virile Saxon despite his Celtic ancestry. In later romances, he, like his nation, shows the influences of French ways and manners. In Malory he presides over the dissolution of his court, and in the sixteenth century he suffers, like other medieval institutions, the indignities brought by the Reformation and Renaissance to England. To that thoroughly Protestant sixteenth-century school-master Roger Ascham the "whole pleasure" of Malory's book "standeth in two special points, in open man-slaughter, and bold bawdry." Thus, Ascham laments the day when "God's Bible was banished the Court, and *Morte Arthure* received into the Prince's Chamber."[1]

Yet even in the sixteenth century, in the midst of the dissolution of monasteries and the destruction of medieval churches, Englishmen "could still feel their pulses quicken at the mention of Arthur,"[2] for no matter how out of sympathy they might be with the "medievalism" of the legend or the ideals of feudal chivalry, their patriotism and national pride, sorely tested during the Hundred Years' War and the Wars of the Roses, made them respond enthusiastically to the memory of the English Arthur. The Tudor kings, moreover, capitalized effectively on the popularity of the Arthur story by sponsoring the great Tudor revival of chivalric customs. Henry VII in stressing his Welsh ancestry meant not only to support his own claim to the throne through the marriage of Katherine the widow of Henry V to Owen Tudor of Wales as well as through his own marriage to Elizabeth of York, but more directly to insinuate that the Tudor line were as blood heirs of Cadwallader, the last truly British king, restorers of the "pristine English glory"[3] of Arthur, whose "blood" had returned, as the prophecies had maintained it would, to rule England. Christening his first son Arthur and naming the child Prince of Wales were visible signs of Henry VII's intent to create by means of deliberate historical antiquarianism an enthusiastic popular allegiance to the Tudor house and a strongly nationalistic policy at home and in Europe.

An interesting barometer of the national feeling on this issue is the reaction among scholars, courtiers, and poets to a history of England written in 1513, though not published until 1543, by Polydore Vergil, a Catholic Italian turned Englishman, in which the humanistic author cast gave doubt upon the historicity of the Arthur of the legends. Despite the logic of his argument and apparent authenticity of his evidence, Polydore Vergil was attacked vehemently by a thoroughly representative group of English Protestant writers—by John Leland, the King's Antiquary, by Arthur Kelton, poet, by John Bale, historian, and by an impressive list of Tudor worthies, all affirming in a tone of outraged dignity the historical reality of Arthur and the blood line that linked him to the Tudor kings.

In spite of this revival of enthusiasm for King Arthur, Malory's book and its French and English sources remained strangely unpopular during the period. Roger Ascham apparently has given us an accurate estimate of Malory's reputation in his time. Nor is this repudiation of the *Morte Darthur* entirely a religious matter: Protestantism continued to use the tradition of the Christian soldier, which was from the time of the Crusades a part of the chivalric tradition and which certainly underlies Malory's conception of heroes like Bors and Gareth. The true interest of the Tudors in Arthur was patriotic rather than chivalric, and the image of the knight as conceived by Henry VII and Henry VIII was related only superficially to the knight of the legend: "The question [in Spenser's time] turned . . . upon the historicity of

Arthur, not upon the quests of his knights or the endless romances that gathered about them to the virtual exclusion of the king, and it is typical of the age that Spenser's Prince Arthur has no counterpart in the legend."[4]

Pleasant as the tournaments, pageants, and banquets of the Tudor monarchs were, none of these kings would ever have imagined that Lancelot or Gawain or even King Arthur could have ruled England effectively in the mid-sixteenth century. The values of knighthood could not have sustained the ruler of a Renaissance state. The "governor," as he was conceived by Elyot, Castiglione, and all the writers of courtesy books, was far more sophisticated, far shrewder, far more complex an individual than any of Malory's knights. For example, the Earl of Surrey, one of the great "silver poets" of the age, seems superficially to fit the mold of the medieval knight; he was an aristocrat, a distinguished soldier, an active courtier, a notable poet. Yet it is impossible to place him in the *Morte Darthur*; he is at home only in the "demedievalized, sophisticated chivalry of Castiglione's *Courtier*."[5] Humanistic learning, though rejected at times as counter to the political and religious *status quo*, had created new values for the courtier-governor-gentleman-prince, values which the chivalric concept of the knight might supplement and grace, but could not replace or threaten seriously.

Chivalry in Tudor England became a romantic vestige of the glorious past, the sort of thing that it will later become, though on a more limited scale and without a strong nationalistic emphasis, in the works of the nineteenth-century Romantic poets. England's enthusiasm for this new romanticized chivalry reached its climax with the crowning of the young Queen Elizabeth in 1558. The poets and writers of the realm, such as Maurice Kyffin, and even the French Pierre de Ronsard stressed her Arthurian descent in order to praise her, and the queen used her Tudor blood to political advantage, to support, for example, her claim to Ireland, and even to demand submission from the Scandanavians on the shaky evidence that Arthur had subdued those Northern lands. The general popularity of the Arthur legend, which had largely subsided during the reigns of the young Edward and Mary, was renewed with vigor during Elizabeth's reign. The Arthurian pageant with which Leicester celebrated the visit of the queen to Kenilworth in 1575, for example, seems to have been but the most extravagant in a series of like entertainments, and there is evidence that there existed a number of London archery societies in which the wealthy and prominent members (including Richard Mulcaster, headmaster of the Merchant Taylor's School during Spenser's tenure there) took the names of the famous Round Table knights.[6]

Yet this enthusiasm was patently contrived, the sort of thing modern Americans love to create in reviving for a town centennial the clothes, the manners, and even the beards of their romantic forbears. In this respect, Stephen Hawes's *The Pastime of Pleasure* deserves some little attention here because it stands after Chaucer and Malory and before Spenser and casts light in both directions; Hawes is, as Arthur Ferguson says, "one of the finest specimens of that perennial hybrid, the 'transitional figure.' "[7] Thus although *The Pastime of Pleasure* utilizes the standard literary devices of the Middle Ages—the dream vision, courtly love, allegory, the chivalric quest—it does so in a new Renaissance spirit of didacticism and romance.

Hawes's great literary model was Lydgate, to whom *The Pastime of Pleasure* is dedicated. The framework and much of the content of *The Pastime*, which deals with the progress of the ideal knight from youth to old age and death, likely came from Lydgate's translation of

De Guilleville's *Le Pèlerinage de la Vie Humaine*, although his use of medieval literary devices reflects a wide acquaintance with the courtly romances. Hawes's purpose is, like Lydgate's, perfectly serious and didactic, "to renue that hath be longe decayd / the floure of chyualry."[8] Hawes is, as W. E. Mead says, an "idealist." "Imbued with the spirit of chivalry so sadly impaired during the brutal Wars of the Roses, he dreams of the perfect knight who, as the perfect lover, wins La Belle Pucell, the perfection of beauty and earthly purity."[9] And although, as Ferguson suggests, the romantic idealism of the poem is tempered by the presence, especially in the treatment of courtly love, of the " 'middle class' values already typical of the English gentry,"[10] we cannot doubt that the poem is essentially idealistic, nostalgic, and instructive.

Yet for all its sententiousness and lack of literary merit, *The Pastime of Pleasure* contributes to our picture of the literary knight during the late fifteenth and early sixteenth centuries. First, Hawes is thoroughly conventional in his approach to and treatment of knighthood; he uses the dream vision, the allegory, courtly love, and the whole panoply of knightly literary regalia because these devices were traditional in his kind of poem. He is, as W. E. Mead says, always describing the "*perfect* knight who, as the *perfect* lover, wins La Belle Pucell, the *perfection* of beauty . . . ," and one sees reflected in Hawes's "perfect," stereotyped, allegorical figures the conventional nature of his work.

The conventionality of Hawes points up the unconventionality of Malory. It is revealing to note that although Hawes had read Malory, there are no perceptible echoes of the *Morte Darthur in The Pastime of Pleasure*.[11] He did not need the Arthur story, of course, but Hawes's chivalry is made up of knights far closer in action and spirit to Chaucer's philosophical Knight, even though they do not share the problems of the various knights of *The Canterbury Tales*, than to Malory's tragic breed. Faced with Hawes's stated didacticism, "to renue that hath be longe decayd / The floure of chyualry," one can see plainly that Malory's purpose in the *Morte Darthur* is no such simple intent and that the sense of corruption and impending tragedy that permeates Malory's book puts to shame the shallow cheeriness of *The Pastime of Pleasure*.

I have stressed Hawes's conventionality here to contrast his book with Malory's, but in one respect Hawes can be called an innovator. Much of the poem, about one-fourth, concerns the education of Graunde Amoure, Hawes's hero. We are given a treatise on the seven liberal arts—grammar, logic, rhetoric, arithmetic, astronomy, music, and geometry. In spite of his difficulties in integrating this material into his plot structure—La Belle Pucell lives in the Tower of Music, and upon winning her love, Graunde Amoure retires to the Tower of Geometry for instruction—Hawes means us to take seriously his injunction to regard these studies as necessary to the training of a knight; although he later receives some training in arms, these liberal studies are the foundation of Graunde Amoure's chivalry.

It thus seems clear that we are in Hawes's poem very close to the "humanism," if we may so misuse the term for a moment, of Chaucer and Spenser and distant from the tragic vision of Malory. Like Chaucer's Knight, Graunde Amoure is both "worthy" and "wys," and although he lacks Chaucer's Knight's philosophical turn of mind, he is certainly far removed from the knights of the romances, who would not have been comfortable, to say the least, in the Tower of Geometry. One cannot say with any assurance that Hawes was influenced by the Knight of *The Canterbury Tales*, but *The Pastime of*

Pleasure certainly seems to reflect, though in a stiff, mechanical fashion, the character of the knight as suggested by Chaucer.

The treatment of courtly love in Hawes's poem shows the same influences. The pattern of courtly love clearly is present (so "medieval" a writer as Hawes naturally would include it), but the emphasis is different. As in the *Franklin's Tale* and Malory's story of Gareth,[12] the bourgeois ideal of marriage replaces the frankly illicit love of the romances, and after a perfectly proper courtship, Graunde Amoure and La Belle Pucell settle down into a comfortable married existence for "ryght many a yere" (5333) until he is cut down in rich old age by "Dethe with his darte" (5384). Like the character of the knight, the doctrine of courtly love has been shaped and altered to fit the secular ideals of the gentry of sixteenth-century England.

But Graunde Amoure is not only the spiritual child of Chaucer's philosophical Knight; he is also the father of Spenser's allegorical questors in *The Faerie Queene*. Later I will make the claim that the "consistently and abstractly allegorical knight is almost totally an invention of Spenser's." The point is here that these pre-Spenserian allegorical knights, like Graunde Amoure, do not represent as do Spenser's figures purely abstract qualities such as Holiness or Magnanimity, but rather stereotyped kinds of knights, generally the Lover. There is a vast difference: Graunde Amoure can act like a human being (though actually he seldom does!); he can be trained, fall in love, marry, grow old, and die, all in a natural and nonallegorical fashion, and although he may come into contact with allegorical figures—Courtesy, Steadfastness, and the like— he himself is not abstractly allegorical in conception, and so remains a figure, like Lancelot or Gawain, with whom the reader can identify. The Spenserian knight, on the other hand, cannot move freely since his actions are determined almost wholly by the allegorical role he must fill.

But despite this difference in allegorical technique, there are similarities in purpose and method between Hawes and Spenser. In their tales of chivalry Hawes and the writers who followed in his tradition, including Spenser, were consciously recreating and romanticizing what they viewed as an archaic system, though as a very lively subject for literature and, most appropriately, for allegory.

Dead ways of life, viewed through the life-giving and transforming lenses of romanticism, frequently spring alive as symbol and allegory, especially in a society which still pays lip service to the code of values that has escaped the grave. The American "Old West" where individualistic heroes might flourish and where an empire might be carved by a strong man has long ceased to exist, yet its image, idealized and romanticized, and its individualistic values, heightened and magnified, are staples of television fare in an industrial America dominated by corporate values and the Madison Avenue vision of the organization man. The grueling hardships of the actual West —the physical discomforts of life on the rawest of frontiers, the crime and immorality of the cattle and mining towns, the constant fear of slaughter by outlaw and Indian—have, of course, faded from the legend leaving only the myth, the purified and allegorized center— the lonely marshal, abandoned by a town, awaiting grimly but indomitably the twelve o'clock train bringing the outlaws pledged to kill him.

Much the same process can be observed in the history of knighthood in Spenser's time. Once the medieval tradition was thoroughly dead, its institutions revamped, its church discredited, its theory and system of government displaced, once "chivalry had . . . lost any embarrassing connection with political or administrative reality,"[13] knighthood might again emerge, not as a reality or as a threat to the Protestant, humanistic *status quo*, but as a literary framework for allegory, a "vehicle for moral instruction in a Protestant and Erastian England."[14]

Spenser's knights are of this new and purely literary sort. He had read the older literature, and to a degree his knights reflect the standards of the early tales; certainly they exhibit honor, prowess, and mercy.[15] But the great central themes and conflicts—between sanctity and chivalry and between loyalty and courtly love—are missing in Spenser, and his knights embody more Renaissance than medieval virtues. The very qualities for which Spenser's knights stand in the allegory—wisdom and temperance, for example—are Renaissance values, totally foreign to the knight of history and to the medieval literary knight as well. Lancelot and Gawain exhibit many virtues, but wisdom and temperance are not among them. It would be alien to Lancelot's nature for him to debate his own behavior as do Spenser's heroes.

Nor is Spenser in creating the knight of *The Faerie Queene* following any historical model, not even the Tudor. His knights resemble neither the primitive warlords, crusaders, and courtly lovers of the early tradition nor the Saxon-killing ancestors of the Tudor kings. *The Faerie Queene* reflects, of course, the adventurous spirit of the Elizabethan age in spite of the "ridiculously archaic"[16] forms of the knights. That is why it is not difficult to see Sidney and Raleigh and Leicester reflected in the "historical allegory" of the poem. But Spenser's knights are not *per se* the courtiers of the English court; they are always envisioned in the archaic trappings of the medieval knights, albeit of a sort that existed neither in history nor in literature, and as such, they speak in long disused formulas.

Nor do Spenser's knights come to him from his major literary sources, the sixteenth-century Italian "romantic epics" of Boiardo, Ariosto, and Tasso. Superficially it is from these poems that he draws the overall structure of *The Faerie Queene*, the patterns of the various adventures, the plot motifs, and even many of the characters; in reading the poem against its sources, one is struck over and over again by Spenser's reliance upon these Italian models. But his knights remain fundamentally different from those of the sources as well as from those of medieval literature and of history, because their allegorical nature determines their forms and actions. One has only to compare Spenser's Britomart with Ariosto's Bradamante, her immediate source, to see the difference and the point. Bradamante in the *Orlando Furioso* is the Renaissance version of the warlike maiden of antiquity, the bold Amazon of the Troy myth. Yet her character in Ariosto is modified by notions of femininity and womanly virtue associated with courtly love and celebrated in Italy by the *dolce stil nuovo* poets and later by Petrarch. She is thus in Ariosto an interestingly rounded character—her tender, delicate heart sharply at odds with her martial, swashbuckling exterior. The same contrast is also evident in *The Faerie Queene*, and those passages where Britomart is troubled by emotions she really does not understand (III, ii, 22 ff.) as well as many of those which show her in battle come to Spenser directly from the *Orlando Furioso*.

Yet Britomart is not Bradamante. Despite the efforts of scholars, mostly working backwards from Spenser, to allegorize all of Ariosto, Bradamante remains only what she is in the action of Ariosto's book, a brilliantly realized character, compared with whom, on the level of action, Britomart "is little better than a big boned country girl."[17] The essence of Britomart in Spenser, on the other hand, lies in her allegorical function. This is not to say that she exists solely for the sake of her allegorical role. But her allegorical role does to a large degree shape and control her character and actions in *The Faerie Queene*, and although the details Spenser received from Ariosto give life and vitality to her characterization, her role as the Knight of Chastity gives meaning to her presence in every situation. Bradamante is chaste, but Britomart is Chastity, chastity conceived by Spenser as an active virtue, "not as abstinence" (for this after all is Belphoebe's role) or even as temperance, but as an "active, honest, and devoted love."[18] Thus her actions seem to be determined first by her allegorical role and then modified by her received character.

Actually the literal and allegorical levels as they exist in a great many passages are well-nigh inseparable; we are not usually conscious of any strain between the necessities of allegory and character. Thus Britomart's destruction of the House of Busirane in Book III is not only allegorically the destruction by Chastity of courtly love or sensual love or whatever the House of Busirane represents, but it is also an action appropriate to the woman we know Britomart to be.

The principle, however, would seem to be that the allegorical need precedes and determines characterization in *The Faerie Queene*. This process can be observed easily in the characters of Books III and IV, as indeed it can in most of the knights, ladies, and monsters in the poem. Spenser's general method in Books III and IV is to define Britomart as Chastity using a series of comparisons and contrasts with various excesses and deficiencies of love, both in men—Braggadochio (cowardly self-love), Olly-

phant (unnatural lust), Malbecco (jealousy and cuckoldry),
Paridell (fickle, adulterous love), Marinell (excessive pa-
rental love), the lustful forester and the witch's son (sly,
bestial passion), the fisherman and Proteus (aged lechery)
—and in women—Florimell (beauty unassisted by other
virtues), Amoret (eager, though restrained passion), Belphoebe (cold, unyielding chastity), Hellenore (promiscuity), and False Florimell (the Petrarchan convention).
Each of these figures, whether fully or sketchily realized
as a character, is first an actor in an allegory, his actions
determined by his role. Thus poor Florimell is forever
facing a fate worse than death because this is a situation
that beauty unprotected by any other virtue cannot avoid.
The jealous, miserly husband (Malbecco) is always in
danger of being forced to choose between love and money
by any handsome passing stranger (Paridell) and so is
cuckolded by a wife (Hellenore) who eventually comes
to prefer promiscuity with satyrs to life with him. This
principle—that allegory determines character and action
in *The Faerie Queene*—is even more evident in those
books, Book I for example, where the allegory is most
pronounced and continuous.

I hope I have not demeaned either the importance of
the story as story in *The Faerie Queene* or that in so emphasizing the allegorical importance of Spenser's characters
I have suggested that *The Faerie Queene* is esoteric and
removed from "real life." Part of the joy in reading Spenser
comes precisely from the enjoyment of incidents and situations on the most literal level. Even in those passages in
which he employs the virtue and vice naming allegorical
method of the Middle Ages, of *The Romance of the Rose*
and *Everyman*—in the Mask of Cupid and the House of
Pride passages, for example—Spenser supplies such a variety
of incident and detail as to make the literal action of the
passage interesting. And throughout *The Faerie Queene*

the allegory is both applicable and true to life, not only for an age, as in *The Romance of the Rose*, but for all time. The tortures of the House of Busirane are universal; they afflict Medea and Lady Brett Ashley, Criseyde and Alice Aisgill alike.

I think, however, that Spenser intended the allegory to govern the book. Sixteenth-century poetry was essentially didactic, and Spenser's statement to Bryskett and the famous letter to Raleigh indicate he intended *The Faerie Queene* to be first of all a book of ethical instruction: "the generall end of all the booke is to fashion a gentleman or noble person in vertuous and gentle discipline." This purpose, similiar to that of the courtesy books, was to be accomplished by allegory, the "darke conceit" of the letter to Raleigh. Spenser's choice of a tale of Arthurian chivalry as a vehicle for allegory was an obvious one: it involved, as nearly all commentators have noted, a fairyland geography and tone suitable for the high adventure Spenser so admired in the romantic Italian epics; it was flexible enough to allow the creation of allegorical characters and incidents; and it could be turned easily, because of its nationalistic and political associations, to the praise of the Queen. As de Selincourt says, the "world of chivalry, which Ariosto viewed for the most part with a sceptical amusement, was to him [Spenser] a reflection of his own ideal conception of conduct, the means through which he might best attain his end, 'to fashion a gentleman or noble person in vertuous and gentle discipline.'"[19] It should strike no one as strange that the allegorical tail wags the legendary dog in *The Faerie Queene*.

This is why Spenser's knights are so different from the other knights of history and literature, even those of his immediate sources. "None of the great knights familiar in Malory and elsewhere appears; none of the great

stories afterward used by Tennyson finds a place."[20] A
great deal too much has perhaps been made of the influence on Spenser of Ariosto's cynical attitude toward the
virtues of chivalry. Scholars debate whether Spenser saw
the cynicism in Ariosto or whether he deliberately mis-
read the *Orlando Furioso* or whether he "corrected"
Ariosto's more flagrantly cynical passages in order to use
the work of his predecessor in what was to be, after all,
a work of ethical instruction. This last theory, I think, is
the most generally held. A comparison of *The Faerie
Queene* with *Orlando Furioso* demonstrates the difference
in tone and method. Graham Hough, for example, after
compiling a list of passages in Book I of *The Faerie
Queene* derived from *Orlando Furioso*, states that in spite
of "all these debts to the Italian epic, of motif, character,
and descriptive detail, we do not feel in Book I that we
are moving in the same world."[21] The adventures of
Orlando Furioso are related for their own sakes, and
Ariosto obviously relishes telling them. "His actors range
from archangels to horses, his scene from Cathay to the
Hebrides."[22] And there is not only plenitude, but variety
of incident and character. The literal in Ariosto is all-
or very nearly all-important, for while there are passages
in *Orlando Furioso*—the Alcena–Logistilla story, for example—which are allegorical, they seem included more
for variety than for instruction.

We must not forget the instructional cast of *The
Faerie Queene*. "Our sage and serious Spenser" was committed by his intention and by the literary practices of his
age to "instruction," and if he were to believe in, or at
least to write about, chivalry at all, it would have to be in
a chivalry uncontaminated by the flippancy of Ariosto:

> O goodly vsage of those antique times,
> In which the sword was seruant vnto right;

When not for malice and contentious crimes,
But all for praise, and proofe of manly might,
The martiall brood accustomed to fight:
Then honour was the meed of victorie,
And yet the vanquished had no despight:
Let later age that noble vse enuie,
Vile rancour to auoid, and cruell surquedrie.

(III, i, 13)

As Padelford points out, the Una–Satyrane–Sansloy–Archi-mago episodes of Book I, contrived by Ariosto "with inimitable mockery of the machinery of chivalry," are treated by Spenser "with grave concern for the moral values of his story."[23]

Ariosto's knights are thus not, any more than are Malory's knights or any actual knights, Spenser's knights, either in character or function. Spenser's knights, as wholly literary creations designed to carry moral and at times political allegory, are unique in the history of literary knighthood up to Spenser's time.[24] Our understanding of *The Canterbury Tales* and of *Sir Gawain and the Green Knight* is enhanced by viewing the knights of these poems against their real-life counterparts, but a comparison of Calidore and Sidney, despite Spenser's probable efforts to identify the two, tells us little about Spenser's knights. John Hughes's remark in 1750 that "the perpetual Stories of Knights, Giants, Castles, and Enchantments, and all that Train of Legendary Adventures, wou'd indeed appear very trifling, if *Spenser* had not found a way to turn all into Allegory"[25] is thus correct, though not perhaps in the sense that Hughes intended it. For although Spenser's basic pattern, as explained in the letter to Raleigh, in which a knight undertakes a given quest, overcomes tremendous obstacles, and eventually wins a lady, comes to him directly from the romances and the behavior of his knights from Plato by way of the humanists and Eliza-

beth's court, their significance is to be found neither in
the romances nor in the humanists nor in the court, but
in the virtues they represent in the poem.

One demonstration of the controlling influence of the
allegorical in Spenser may be seen in the chivalric pattern
of Book I. The question of the chronology of the various
books of the poem is of almost no importance here.
Although Book I was almost certainly composed after
Books III and IV and differs from those earlier books in
having a purer, a more classical chivalric pattern of action,
its treatment of the legend is not different from that of
the other books, although, as Dodge so carefully has
shown, Spenser's allegory in *The Faerie Queene* becomes
less mechanical as the poem progresses.[26]

The pattern of action in Book I eventually is derived
from that of the so-called "Fair Unknown" group of
romances—e.g. the English *Lybius Desconus*, the French
Le Bel Inconnu, the German *Wigalois*, and the "Tale
of Gareth" in Malory's *Morte Darthur*. The basic pattern
of these romances is nearly identical, though details may
vary from version to version. A young knight of unknown
though noble origin comes to Arthur's court seeking
adventure. There he is scorned, usually by Kay, and
given menial tasks. After a time, however, he is permitted
to take up the quest of freeing a noblewoman from either
imprisonment or enchantment, often in the form of a
serpent. Although he is ridiculed by the lady's messenger
(often her sister or maid-in-waiting), he eventually con-
quers his foes and rescues and marries the imprisoned lady.

Spenser's Red Cross Knight resembles the Fair Unknown in a number of superficial ways: the Red Cross
Knight, like Gareth a "clownish young man," has come
to Arthur's court seeking adventure; the quest to rescue
Una's parents from the "Old Dragon" is his first quest;
he is accompanied by a relative of the person to be

rescued; Una several times warns the Red Cross Knight of approaching danger; he must eventually overcome a great force and endure a period of delay to marry the lady. These similarities are broad, and commentators agree that Spenser borrows from his sources only the elementary structure of the tale and that differences in treatment are more numerous and more striking than similarities.[27] Certainly the older stories do not equal the variety of opponents encountered by the Red Cross Knight. The opponents of the young knight in Spenser's sources hardly are distinguishable from each other. To be sure, there are the three avenging brothers, the use of which in Spenser already has been analyzed,[28] and the usual complement of giants, magicians, and sorceresses, but nothing in any of the stories suggests Spenser's use of Archimago, Duessa, Fraelissa, Fradubio, Abessa, Corceca, Kirkrapine, Orgoglio, and Charissa, not to mention his conception of a superhero in Prince Arthur. This variety stems directly not from the dictates of the narrative, but from the allegory. As long as the reader's, or listener's, major interest lay in the incidents themselves and not in their significance, then only the incidents—the manner of meetings between knights, the details of combat, etc.—were subject to variation. In adapting the pattern of the ancient tale of the Fair Unknown as a vehicle for allegory, Spenser individualized the generic, characterless opponents of his sources to give them allegorical places. Thus, the three avenging brothers become Sansloy, Sansfoy, and Sansjoy, not simply avengers but characters in the allegory opposed by their very natures to Holiness in search of Faith. The witless giants of the sources become Orgoglio, the looming figure of spiritual pride; the magicians become Archimago, Hypocrisy; the sorceresses Duessa, Duplicity; and the dragon, Death or Sin. The allegory demands, however, more opponents to

Holiness than the sources can supply, so Spenser created Fidessa (Little Faith), Fraelissa (Frailty), Fradubio (Doubt), Abessa (Superstition), Corceca (Blind Devotion), and Kirkrapine (Abuse of Church).

The allegory of *The Faerie Queene* demands that place as well as character be individualized. There is little description of place as place in the medieval romances. We see mentioned Logres or Brittany or even Winchester, but a town in the romances is simply "a town" and a castle is only "a castle." The Renaissance Italian writers were more lavish with geographical detail, but in a purely superficial way; their descriptions are simply attempts to lend verisimilitude at the level of physical action. Neither technique was useful to Spenser because neither could contribute to allegory. Thus, he creates in Book I an allegorically-conceived House of Pride, which in its architecture and evil practices encompasses all the traps into which Pride may lead a weak, though good-intentioned, Holiness which has lost its Faith, and an allegorically-conceived House of Holiness, where natural Holiness may rearm itself for its coming battle with Sin and Death. As with the use of character, allegory has here dictated narrative and demanded a literary technique different from that of the sources.

My point is that Spenser takes from his sources only the barest suggestion of a pattern, an incident, the shape of a character. The fleshing out, the creative work of the imagination, is dictated by the allegory, by the *sens* which the traditional, but reformed *matière* must carry. This is what I think Janet Spens means by calling *The Faerie Queene* a "philosophical poem,"[29] that the philosophy came first and largely dictated the form and matter of the poem. The philosophy of love, for example, occupied a place of great importance in Elizabethan court life and in the chivalric romances and is quite naturally reflected

in *The Faerie Queene*.[30] Books III and IV are completely given over to it. But how different is Spenser's
treatment of love from Malory's, Chrétien's, or even
Ariosto's. Love in Spenser is first of all Platonic love:

> Most sacred fire, that burnest mightily
> In liuing brests, ykindled first aboue
> Emongst th' eternall spheres and lamping sky,
> And thence pourd into men, which men call Loue;
> Not that same, which doth base affections moue
> In brutish minds, and filthy lust inflame,
> But that sweet fit, that doth true beautie loue,
> And choseth vertue for his dearest Dame,
> Whence spring all noble deeds and neuer dying fame.
>   (III, iii, I)

Love in Spenser is thus of heavenly, never earthly birth,
and though it may be at times, "in brutish minds,"
expended on material objects, its true nature is to seek
out spiritual objects. Allegorically in the poem Magnificence (Arthur) is seeking Glory (Gloriana). But the
poem makes plain that Gloriana (who represents also
Queen Elizabeth), however great her attributes, is not
herself the Glory that Magnificence is seeking, but only
one embodiment of it. True Glory, actually the object of
Arthur's love, must be sought for and loved in its pure
and noumenal state, never confused with any earthly and
temporary embodiment.

Nothing could be farther from the medieval and
chivalric view. The lady herself, not her spiritual qualities,
is the object of the medieval courtly lover, and even
though the late stages of the troubadour tradition yield to a
degree of spiritualization in the *dolce stil nuovo* poets and
especially in Dante, the tradition of Arthurian literature
before Spenser, except perhaps in Malory,[31] seems to extol
the virtues of courtly love, which, in spite of its spiritual-

izing effects upon the lover, culminates in physical embrace.

C. S. Lewis has pointed out that much of Book III, and particularly the Mask of Cupid which Britomart witnesses at the House of Busirane, is a condemnation of courtly love and records the final literary defeat of the ideal of courtly love by the ideal of marriage.[32] Spenser is seen by Lewis as overcoming "the desperate medieval split between *amour courtois* and the severity of the Christian scheme of redemption."[33] I think Lewis is essentially correct in his interpretation of the House of Busirane as Spenser's condemnation of courtly love, though no one, including Lewis, would agree that it is only that. Book III is full of false loves and lovers—the six stages of carnal love represented by the Knights of Castle Joyous, the sly, bestial passion of the lustful forester, the aged lechery of the fisherman and Proteus, the unnatural lust of Ollyphant, the jealous cuckoldry of Malbecco, the fickle adultery of Paridell, the unbridled passion of Hellenore—all these and more, and various kinds of true love seen in Florimell, Amoret, and Belphoebe; and Book IV, with its distinction between "deare affection unto kindred sweet," "raging fire of love to woman kind," and "zeale of friends combyned with vertues meet," (ix, 1), continues the examination of love begun in Book III. But the point is that all of Spenser's presentation of love, specifically Platonic love, in these two books is handled not through discussion and commentary but through the action of allegory. Each kind of love, each type of relationship has its appropriate allegorical representative and incident, and Spenser demonstrates, again by means of character and incident, the immense complexity of the possible relationships in which men and women find themselves.

A brief comparison of the technique of Books III and

IV of *The Faerie Queene* with any of the romances of
Chrétien is instructive. Chrétien's subject is also love,
more particularly courtly love. Chrétien's treatment of
love is thus far more limited in scope than is Spenser's.
Spenser, in spite of his variety, demonstrates a single
point: he is everywhere praising the Renaissance concepts
of Platonic love and friendship, the blending of spirits and
communion of souls between those of equal abilities and
qualities. As William Schofield says, he is intent on
uniting in these books "pagan philosophy with Puritan
morality."[34] Chrétien, unlike Spenser, is no allegorist, and
so whatever *sens* appears in Chrétien is contained *within*
the *matière*, not appended to it. We read the *Erec* or the
Yvain or the *Lancelot*, and having finished the romance
and examined it, we discover in retrospect its implications. Chrétien's narrative is symbolic only occasionally,
and the reader must struggle with the meaning of the
whole poem, not with an accumulation of its parts.

In reading Spenser, however, one must deal first with
the parts, because it is there that Spenser begins. We
must interpret as we go, and although when we have
finished, we can with little difficulty establish the larger
meaning of the whole, we have had to arrive at it by
fitting together the myriad allegorical pieces of character
and incident that Spenser has composed so carefully
for us.

A comparison of Chrétien's treatment of love with
that of Spenser also demonstrates the latter's relation to
the myth of knighthood. The romances of Chrétien in
dealing with the complex and bitter ethical struggles of
actual chivalry—the dilemmas of Christ vs. Venus, feudal
lord vs. lady, duty vs. love—reflect the central myth of all
knighthood, the journey of the hero from innocence to
knowledge, from the "ephemeral and illusory to reality
and eternity." Chrétien's works thus assume a meaning

and relevance to life far greater than the episodic adventures of their heroes might suggest. Spenser's allegories by treating the knight simply as a literary device deliberately avoid the realities of knighthood and so fail to reflect the myth of the hero. We can thus read *The Faerie Queene* consistently on literal and allegorical levels, but we can go no farther. The figures of the lovers of Book III are meticulously drawn; they chart brilliantly a catalogue of the effects of passion, and we are expected to see in them nearly all the varieties of human love allegorically described. But the chart suggests nothing beyond itself; once constructed, it is self-contained and complete.

In Chrétien's romances there are no charts, no schematizations of passion. But in dealing with situations, however fancifully presented, and people, however idealized, rather than with allegorical units, and by utilizing unconsciously the already meaningful pattern of the hero myth, Chrétien suggests an anagogical level because of its range and universality of far more significance to the human predicament than that of Spenser's limited allegories. The trials and eventual redemption of Erec or Yvain, despite their cloak of romance, present by reference to the realities of myth the circumstances of human love more fully and more accurately than do Spenser's measured allegories. The relation of vehicle to tenor in allegory is always simply one to one: Ollyphant is lust but only lust, Proteus lechery but only lechery. In myth, as in symbol, the numerical relationship is one to infinity, and Yvain becomes Everyman engaged in the quest of finding a mature relationship with the world.

I do not intend to disparage Spenser's great accomplishment in the poem. Allegory requires great skill, and it is Spenser's greatest glory that he can avoid the mechanical lifelessness which too often infests even carefully planned allegory. But the allegory does come first

in *The Faerie Queene* as it does not in Chrétien and
Malory, and it dictates completely the concept of the
knight in the poem. Spenser's knights, whatever their
characters, whether as virtuous as Calidore or as foul
and vain as Braggadochio, are in service of the allegory.
One cannot imagine any of Chrétien's or Malory's knights
undergoing the humiliations or defeats which the Red
Cross Knight must suffer and yet emerging victorious.
For most of Book I, the Red Cross Knight acts in a most
unknightly fashion—duped by Archimago, taken in by
Duessa, almost enslaved by Pride, captured by Orgoglio—
but his failures are necessary because the allegory demands
them; we must witness the difficulties into which Holiness,
separated from the true Faith, can fall. Even Calidore,
who represents Courtesy, engages in a most unchivalric
pastoral sojourn because the allegory of courtesy demands
that Spenser show that true *gentillesse* is based not only
on court training and gentle birth, but also on "natural"
gentility bestowed by God, a concept best, and traditionally, portrayed by the use of an arcadian setting. It is
impossible to imagine Lancelot or any of the great Elizabethan courtiers in such a situation, but that is not the
point.[35] Spenser's knights have no character or characteristics as knights: they are derived neither from history
nor from books; they are figures in an allegory, and they
move by the dictates of the allegory.

It is impossible, therefore, to place Spenser's knights
in relation to any connected history of literary knighthood
or to the myth of the hero-knight since they have no
definite qualities in themselves. They exhibit the stylized
qualities of the type, and it would be possible to list their
attributes—prowess, courtesy, kindness, etc.[36] But to present these characteristics as a picture of the Spenserian
knight would be misleading, for it would obscure the
shifting, allegorical use of Spenser's knights in *The Faerie*

Queene. Spenser's knights, like his language, are deliberately archaic: by Spenser's time they no longer resembled anything in nature or in life. The figure of the knight will from the time of *The Faerie Queene* onward become increasingly a purely literary figure, a legend of the past, and like most legends, destined to lose both its proper shape and its touch with reality.

THE LAST KNIGHTS

SHAKESPEARE AND AFTER

WITH *The Faerie Queene* the major part of this study comes to a natural end; for with *The Faerie Queene* the knight became a purely literary figure, which since it no longer reflected any living reality was no longer capable of development but only of use. While chivalry was changing, literary knighthood had changed with it, and even the most cursory reader can discern the basic differences in thought and action that separate Roland from Chaucer's Knight and Lancelot. He would agree, I think, on studying the relevant historical texts that these differences were to a degree caused by changes in the concept of knighthood during the five hundred years involved. To present the matter at its most obvious, the doctrines of courtly love presented Lancelot with a set of problems to which Roland was mercifully oblivious. As long as there was any historical reality to adhere to, the portraits of the knights in literature adhered to it, albeit they also interpreted it. Even Chaucer's paragon reflects, though from a variety of prisms, the living knight of the fourteenth century, and the very fleshlessness of Spenser's knights reveals the thin chivalric covering of the Renaissance courtier.

I deliberately have limited this study to those major writers whose knights bore some relation to the actual chivalry of their times. Naturally, not all medieval writers of romance had Chrétien's or the *Gawain*-poet's gifts. Stereotyped, conventionalized chivalric literature existed throughout the period from Chrétien to Spenser. Names such as Manessier, Ulrich von Zatzikhoven, Kyot (if he existed), or, much later, Sir Gilbert Hay and Adam Loutful mean little now, even to literary historians, yet these and many others were faithful chroniclers and translators of gallant deeds of countless chivalric heroes. In relying upon types and conventions, however, these men reflected in their works nothing of the living chivalry around them, but only the pleasant distortions and popular images with which the people of that age charmed themselves.

Their closeness to the problems of actual life brings Chrétien and the others close to the themes and images of myth. For, paradoxically, the farther away one gets from mere surface and the closer to the meaning, the "reality" of an action, the closer one draws to its myth. This closeness to the heart of the action is, for example, what makes Faulkner's *The Bear* the best hunting story and *Moby Dick* the best fishing yarn ever written. Yet they are also the most mythic hunting and fishing stories ever told, as the criticism devoted to them proves. The same thing is true of the literature we have examined. Myth is relevant to *Sir Gawain and the Green Knight* not because the *Gawain*-poet put it in the poem, but because in approaching the truth about the chivalric quest, he ran headlong into its myth. The "traditionalist" romancers in avoiding the conflicts and dilemmas which lay at the heart of chivalry avoided its meaning as well.

Let me make the point another way. Courtly love, or

at least the debate about courtly love, was the chief amusement of the French aristocracy of the thirteenth and fourteenth centuries. Like the circuses of the later Roman days or the various "charity" occasions of our own, it occupied a decadent society with pleasantries that could be justified as somehow useful, even ennobling. And it is true that courtly love civilized the armed crusader and in a sense created chivalry. Yet it was also corrupt, condemned by the church for its flagrant championing of adultery and female sovereignty. Thus, the knight who espoused and followed, as his society doubtless expected him to do, the precepts and practices of courtly love could not hope to remain a soldier of Christ as he had sworn to do. He could not even expect to be buried in holy ground. He was thus presented in life with an irreconcilable dilemma which must have, if he were at all sensitive, caused him extreme anguish.

Chrétien reflects this terrible dilemma which courtly love forced upon the knight and so do *Sir Gawain and the Green Knight, The Franklin's Tale,* and the *Morte Darthur.* But the majority of medieval romances do not touch upon it, nor, for a different reason, does Spenser. The romances that have come down to us, written in half a dozen languages and representing the work of an unknown number of writers, are all of a piece. "One day whilst Arthur was dining in his hall," they all begin, and there follows the usual pageant of chivalric exploits, differing from one another only in minor detail.

Their involvement with the underlying conflicts of knighthood, the tensions and strains of its divided loyalties to King, to Church, to Lady, separates the writers we have dealt with from these mere romancers, and the changes in emphasis in these basic chivalric conflicts—for they never really wholly disappear—cause the knight to develop as a literary character from Roland to Arveragus. For Roland these problems do not exist; he is capable of perfect loyalty to King and Church, and Lady hardly enters the poem. Chrétien's Erec and Yvain feel the first tugs of the tension that will later destroy Malory's court; both for a time are unfaithful—Erec to knighthood, Yvain to love—though both are able in the end to piece together all their loyalties, exactly as Chaucer's Arveragus will do later, within the framework of Christian marriage. Yet only a little later, Gawain, the best knight in the French romances—although he lies, makes a false confession to a priest, and flinches from a blow—is judged because of his humility, willingness to face the truth about himself, and ultimate adherence of his knightly vows to be infinitely superior to the proud court, which, although corrupt, refuses to see the relevance of what Gawain has learned. And the outcome of the court's blindness, the failure of chivalry to realize its own inherent weaknesses, is exactly the point of Chaucer's examination of the knight and the theme of Malory's great tragedy.

But with Malory, the literary progress of chivalry, which is a kind of allegorical history of man from innocence to tragedy, comes to its natural end and with it its myth. *The Faerie Queene*, though it deals superficially with some of knighthood's conflicts, does not treat the knight as an innocent or as a tragic failure or as anything in between. For Spenser's knights are not knights at all, but merely pegs on which to hang allegories; their knighthood is irrelevant to their characters. And Spenser in this way points toward the future of literary knighthood.

Spenser, like the Tudor kings, at least upheld an image of the past glory of the institution of chivalry. Yet Shakespeare's knights—Sir Toby Belch, Sir Andrew Aguecheek, Sir John Falstaff—show to what depths the general concept of knighthood had sunk during the later years of the sixteenth century.

Certainly the point seems worth making. For whatever these degenerate knights—drunken, corrupt, cynical—may have in common with Sir Dagonet and Sir Dinadan, the laughers and japers of Malory's book,[1] it is impossible to imagine their occupying a remotely sympathetic place in any medieval or early Renaissance work. Braggadochio in *The Fairie Queene* is unbelievably corrupt, yet he is roundly condemned, and we sympathize with Red Cross Knight's unknightly behavior at the House of Pride only because we are sure he will rise above these excesses later on. But although Falstaff eventually perishes, Sir Toby, complete with cakes and ale, triumphs over Malvolio, and it is clear that in spite of his presentation of the great knights of the history plays Shakespeare had no interest in upholding traditional notions of knightly conduct.

The two *Henry IV* plays certainly demonstrate that even in the history plays Shakespeare was not concerned with glorifying the heroic chivalry of the past. Henry V is, of course, *the* great knight in every respect, but the progress of his education in the *Henry IV* plays shows clearly enough that Hal rises to chivalric perfection within a diseased society, a nation ungoverned and unbridled. His father, Henry IV, a thoroughly "modern" man, comes to the throne by destroying the values of the older code; whatever Richard's weaknesses, he had at least represented and remained true to the stable chivalric values of the medieval tradition—loyalty, the divine right of monarchs, Christian knighthood. Henry IV is another sort of man: Hotspur calls him a "vile politician," and he is essentially just that—manipulating other men skillfully and expeditiously for his own purposes. In the end, in *2 Henry IV* the king comes to know himself and the "by-paths and

indirect crookt ways" by which he "snatched with bois-
t'rous hand" the throne of England, but he is by then
ruler of a degenerate and demoralized court and land.
Hal has returned to the Boar's Head after his brief glory
at Shrewsbury; Hotspur, in whom there was at least health
and vigor, is dead; Falstaff is old and with age has come
desperation—he is afflicted with "more diseases than he
knew of"; a new group of rebels led by the Archbishop of
York now plagues the king.

Shakespeare meant to show by all this the afflictions
that accompany the deposition of a rightful king—a king,
by the way, whose faults forgiven, has now become a
martyr: "they that, when Richard lived, would have him
die / Are now become enamoured on his grave." Renaissance political theory still held strongly the doctrine of
the divine right of Christian kings, and Shakespeare's
audience would see the troubles of Henry as stemming
from his usurpation of Richard's throne. But there is
more to 2 *Henry IV* than the misfortunes of a man who
has violated a principle of politics. Henry IV had put to
death at Pomfret a pattern of life and a set of values;
with Richard had perished the unquestioned faith of
medieval man in the rightness and inevitability of chivalric
government and conduct. The "victory" of Prince John of
Lancaster over the rebels in Gaultree Forest is as carefully
planned, as shrewdly managed, and as palpably modern
in conception and execution as any coup of modern
diplomacy. Yet it would be difficult to find a less heroic,
less honorable, less chivalric victory managed by modern
statesmen, let alone by a group of Christian knights.
In a way, Prince John is a natural extension of his father
and of his father's way of doing things.

Hal is a different breed of man, and in the policies
and deeds of Henry V there is perceptible something of
Hotspur and Poins, of Falstaff and the Lord Chief Justice,

as well as the shadow of Henry IV. Hal's receiving of
the crown:

> My gracious liege,
> You won it, wore it, gave it me;
> Then plain and right must my possession be;
> Which I with more than with a common pain
> 'Gainst all the world will rightfully maintain.

is no casual acceptance of a token right, but the considered undertaking of a prince carefully prepared for
responsibility. And in that responsibility and the new
order and polity for England that grows out of it, there
remains much of the chivalric code of Richard, strength-
ened, transformed, and fitted to the new age by the
rounded education of Hal, but still to be seen in the
king's gallantry at Harfleur, in his relations with nobles
and commons alike at Agincourt, and in his courtship of
Katharine.

Harry's knighthood, however, is not the point of the
play—Harry is; and in that distinction alone one sees that
Shakespeare is not bound to uphold or depict any
special concept of the knight. In fact, Hal, Henry IV,
Falstaff, Hotspur, and Prince John of Lancaster are all
knights; yet the differences in their conduct are surely
more pronounced than are the similarities. This study,
however, is not so much concerned with what Shakespeare
did with the traditional figure of the knight, but with the
point that by Shakespeare's time such shabby knights
could appear and their actions be condoned in literature
at all and, incidentally, that they should appear in Shakespeare, but not in Spenser. The second of these two
propositions is the easier to deal with. Spenser was at
times a courtier himself, on intimate terms with the court
group for which he wrote, and *The Faerie Queene* was
written to define and promote a system of aristocratic

values best illustrated and symbolized by the traditional concept of the knight. For although Spenser allowed his conception of particular knights and of knighthood in general to be determined largely by his allegory, he extols throughout *The Faerie Queene* the general values of chivalry. There are "bad" knights in Spenser, to be sure, but they are everywhere condemned.

Shakespeare, whatever his private ambitions, certainly had no chivalric bias. A knight, like a duke or a clergyman, was to him simply a character in a play, whether noble like old Sir Thomas Erpingham, corrupt and an evil influence like Falstaff, or corrupt himself yet a destroyer of a worse evil like Sir Toby Belch. The knight as knight, whatever the variations in his character, exists in Spenser as a model for instruction; in Shakespeare he does not exist at all.

Thus, although the same historical and literary forces were at work upon both Spenser and Shakespeare, their different literary purposes caused them to use the tradition of knighthood differently. Arthur Ferguson remarks that England under Elizabeth "again sought inspiration . . . in the legends of Arthur's court and . . . in the chivalric code an ethical form for life in a new and swashbuckling society."[2] This reaffirmation of chivalry may well have been part of Spenser's purpose in *The Faerie Queene*, the very means by which he thought to "fashion a gentleman or noble person in vertuous and gentle discipline." But it was certainly not part of Shakespeare's reason for writing. In fact, one of Shakespeare's chief glories is that in electing to see life steadily and whole, he never attempts to judge or try to reform it.

Shakespeare thus makes use of a historical and literary type, the corrupt knight, denied to Spenser by his purpose in writing. Likely the type already existed in literature for Shakespeare to use. Chaucer had ridiculed the knight

—though not the ideals he served—in *Sir Thopas* two centuries before Shakespeare's time, and the courtesy manuals of the fifteenth and sixteenth centuries provide many admonitions, observed in living offenders, against the abuses of the knightly code: "Because a knight being without harness, and that hath no riches for to make his dispences, if he be made knight, him should peradventure hap for need to be a robber, a thief, traitor, liar or beguiler, or have some other vices which be contrary to chivalry—a man lame, or over great, or over fat, or that hath any other evil disposition in his body, is not sufficient to be a knight."[3] The Church, not content with criticizing the practices of knighthood, condemned its idealistic code as well.[4] And most importantly, chivalry by Shakespeare's time had become food for satire by outliving its usefulness; it no longer bore any relation to the conduct of life. Even a hundred years before Shakespeare's birth, "the most effective intellectual force operating against the chivalric ideal in the later fifteenth century [had been] the spirit of undoctrinaire realism, of practicality and good sense, that becomes increasingly apparent in the political literature of that era. . . ."[5] Certainly by the sixteenth century all occasions informed against the chivalric code: "the humanism of Henry VIII's reign and that of his son represented an especially sharp break with the chivalric tradition. . . . Their world was, in fact, a new world in which the medieval knight was himself quite out of place."[6] The new dramatic literature of the late sixteenth century, which like the drama in every age reflected social changes more quickly than did other genres and which unlike other literary forms in the sixteenth century was not essentially instructional, tended to use the knight dramatically and realistically rather than didactically and inspirationally.

This same point can be made by a brief review of a

parallel literary circumstance, the progress of the Petrarchan convention in Elizabethan poetry. Originally imported into English literature as a source of new techniques of poetic form (the sonnet), language (the use of conceits and figures), and subject matter (the serious treatment of love through wit and paradox), the Petrarchan sonnet soon became because of its variety and range the most seriously regarded form of Elizabethan poetry. "The problem was to make love seem an almost heroic subject, and to do it by the consuming nature of the [lover's] experience. The lover within the poetry had to reflect the world outside him, had to make that world seem relevant to, and involved in, what was after all only his own individual state of mind. This could be done by metaphors . . . ,"[7] and it resulted in a number of conventions, highly stylized mannerisms both of verse technique and of subject matter—e.g., the use of paradoxes and contraries and of elaborate and at times strained conceits drawn from all areas of science and learning, the cruelty of the lady and patient devotion of the lover, the stylized descriptions of the lady (hair like wires, lips like corals, etc.), the sonnet cycle depicting the whole progress of courtship, the Platonic identification of beauty and virtue with its attendant emphasis upon the lady's spiritual qualities. Thus the Petrarchan convention soon established itself in English verse as treating in stylized forms an idealized pattern of love derived from courtly love, though generally lacking courtly love's emphasis upon adultery.

The Petrarchan convention because of its idealism and its ties with the Middle Ages was like the ideal of chivalry open to the attacks of the "spirit of undoctrinaire realism" that virtually destroyed the chivalric values of the fifteenth and sixteenth centuries. And just as Shakespeare's shabby knights satirize, consciously or unconsciously, the pre-

tensions of chivalry, so occasionally there operates within
the Petrarchan sonnet itself the satiric counterspirit of
"undoctrinaire realism." "My mistress' eyes are nothing
like the sun" begins one of Shakespeare's sonnets (130)
and then proceeds to satirize one by one the strained
comparisons of the Petrarchan ideal:

> My mistress' eyes are nothing like the sun;
> Coral is far more white than her lips red;
> If snow be white, why then her breasts are dun;
> If hairs be wires, black wires grow on her head.
> I have seen roses damask'd, red and white,
> But no such roses see I in her cheeks;
> And in some perfumes is there more delight
> Than in the breath that from my mistress reeks.
> I love to hear her speak, yet well I know
> That music hath a far more pleasing sound;
> I grant I never saw a goddess go—
> My mistress when she walks treads on the ground.
>   And yet, by heaven, I think my love as rare
>   As any she belied with false compare.

Similar evidences of anti-Petrarchan feeling can be found
in the sonnets of Sir John Davies and others,[8] and the
figure of False Florimell in *The Faerie Queene* is almost
certainly meant to represent the lady of the Petrarchan
tradition, here stripped of the inner grace which normally
in the tradition accompanies and gives meaning to the
outer beauty:

> In stead of eyes two burning lampes she [the witch] set
> In siluer sockets, shyning like the skyes,
> And a quicke mouing Spirit did arret
> To stirre and roll them, like a womans eyes;
> In stead of yellow lockes she did deuise,
> With golden wyre to weaue her curled head;

Yet golden wyre was not so yellow thrise
As Florimells faire haire: and in the stead
Of life, she put a Spright to rule the carkasse dead.

                              (III, viii, 7)

Although Spenser's purpose in describing False Florimell
in these terms is clearly not to satirize either the poetic
forms or the Platonic ideas of the Petrarchan convention,
the presentation here of False Florimell and her actions
in the rest of the poem do demonstrate that the mannerisms of the Petrarchan mode, like the mannerisms of
knighthood, were, as time and belief in the ideas behind
the convention passed, separated from the values which
they had originally illustrated and hence were held up
for mockery and scorn.

The knight of literature, divorced from both reality
and myth from the time of Spenser and Shakespeare
onward, thus became more and more of a purely literary
device used to portray whatever vices or virtues were
demanded of him. *Don Quixote*, for example, exhibits
both sides of the coin by satirizing the literature of knighthood and at the same time using the figure of the knight,
divorced from any sort of historical context, as a con-
venient fictional device to present the complex interaction
of appearance and reality that is its major theme. The
fortunes of the Arthurian legend will serve well to mark
the use of the literary knight in post-medieval English
literature. And in the seventeenth and eighteenth centuries those fortunes were low indeed. Roberta Florence
Brinkley after a thorough survey is forced to conclude
that "the study of the Arthurian legend in the seventeenth
century has revealed almost no romance."[9] For although
Jonson, Dryden,[10] and Milton planned at some time in
their careers epic treatments of the Arthur legend, only
the poetaster Sir Richard Blackmore treated the legend

in the style of the times, in neoclassical epic terms, adapting in general Spenser's scheme of organizing his book around a treatment of the Aristotelian virtues, but viewing the whole legend in most unmedieval terms as a religious and political allegory in which Arthur plainly represents William of Orange defending Protestant England against its Catholic foes. It is instructive also that Milton finally rejected the Arthurian legend, which he had considered for years, as the subject of the great poem for which he so arduously had trained himself. His exact reasons for doing so are past knowing, but Milton presumably was influenced by the Trojan-Saxon controversy over the origins of British history, what Douglas Bush calls the "slow death of the matter of Brute, New Troy, and Arthur"[11] at the hands of the new, scientific historiography. And although he was probably led by his Puritan faith to distrust all legend, the best guess is still that he simply decided that the tales of Arthur and the Round Table, no matter how pleasant or how attractive they might be to him as a writer, were in the end not heroic, weighty, or moral enough for the highly serious poem he planned to write.[12] The famous passage in Book IX of *Paradise Lost* in which he repudiates as fit subjects for epic verse "Races and Games, / Or tilting Furniture, emblazond Shields, / Impresses quaint, Caparisons and Steeds: / Bases and tinsel trappings, gorgious Knights / At Joust and Torneament; then marshald Feast / Serv'd up in Hall and Servers, and Seneshals" demonstrates clearly enough Milton's disillusionment with the Arthurian past.

My intention has not been to write anything like a connected history of literary knighthood, and there is little point in my continuing this account of the fortunes of chivalry into more recent literary history. There are certainly numerous excellent studies of the knight, and more particularly of the Arthurian legend, in the literature of the nineteenth and twentieth centuries, all of which make essentially the point that I have been making in the past few pages, that the knight, after the death of the institution of knighthood, became an empty vessel, a literary mannequin bearing like any other purely literary creation no relation to any reality beyond that inherited and malleable image carried about by all of us from youthful readings of various tales of King Arthur. Thus, the literary knight comes to "mean" whatever his creator wishes him to "mean": to Tennyson a standard of conduct for Victorian England; to E. A. Robinson a psychologically confused and skeptical modern; to John Erskine a degraded and cynical hypocrite; to Charles Williams the Christian soul in search of salvation; to T. H. White an antique version of the British national character; and to all of these, as to dozens more modern authors who have treated the legend, a figure to show forth the times, whether for praise or for condemnation.

But for none of these, not even for those most in sympathy with its values, like Charles Williams or T. S. Eliot, is the myth of knighthood quite real or its ethical dilemmas the center of life. From the eleventh through the fifteenth centuries, chivalry was in varying degrees an operative mode of life, an ethic, and the myth of the questing hero the natural means of its expression. We can trace in the literature of the period the moral fortunes of knighthood from its unquestioned and unquestioning self-assuredness in *The Song of Roland* through the first intimations of its moral uncertainty in Chrétien, the foreshadowings of its failure in *Sir Gawain and the Green Knight*, its sublimation into bourgeois morality in Chaucer to its final tragic decline in Malory. And in all of these there is present a sense of urgency, no mere use of the knight as a literary device but a concern for the morality of knighthood itself. As long as this concern for the ethics of chivalry remained, the questing myth remained also in a variety of forms as its vehicle, a means of growth in Chrétien, a test in *Sir Gawain and the Green Knight*, a means of organization in *The Canterbury Tales*, an unapproachable ideal in Malory. The myth is, as one would expect, strongest in Chrétien, weakest in the later works in which its patterns had become vestigial, and from Spenser onward, almost nonexistent.

The presence of the myth of knighthood in these writers' works thus reflects their involvement with the morality of chivalry. Through the myth of the questing hero, mere historical knighthood was by them elevated and given a meaning and a universality beyond itself; "history was regenerated, for it was in fact the revivification, the reactualization of a primordial heroic myth."[13] And although the myth outlived the historical event, it soon, stripped of any factual referent, lost its relevance and its power. The "new" Arthurian works, even the best of them, are using as symbols and tokens the realities of an older age; and their deliberate archaisms, their Lancelots and Gawains, only intensify the immediacy of Chrétien's Erec and Malory's Gareth.

But the literature of chivalry itself, in the old books which record its proper shape and form, still retains its freshness and its strength. Like the great cathedrals, it is both a monument to a past age and a living witness to the timelessness of man's achievement.

NOTES

INTRODUCTION

[1] *Sir Gawain and the Green Knight,* tr. Theodore Banks, Jr. (New York: F. S. Crofts and Co., Inc., 1929), ll. 2414-19.

[2] I accept, as will almost any serious reader, the argument that the initiation, *rite de passage,* withdrawal-return pattern underlies the poem and directs its structure and theme.

[3] "Sir Gawain and the Green Knight," *Scrutiny,* XVI (1949), 274-300.

[4] For discussion of medieval allegory, see such primary sources as Dante's *Letter to Can Grande,* Boccaccio's *Vita di Dante,* and St. Thomas Aquinas' commentary in *Summa Theologica,* I, p. 11, a. 10, and such modern works as C. S. Lewis' *The Allegory of Love* (London: Oxford University Press, 1936), Karl Vossler's *Medieval Culture,* 2 vols. (New York: Macmillan Co., 1929), and Henri de Lubac's *Exégèse Médiévale* (Paris: Aubier, 1959), and the discussions in *Critical Approaches to Medieval Literature* (New York: Columbia University Press, 1960).

[5] For full discussions of the elements of the basic initiation-quest pattern, the reader is directed to those volumes devoted to defining and analyzing the pattern as it appears in myth and primitive custom, particularly to Van Gennep's *Les Rites de Passage* (Paris: E. Nourry, 1909), and to works interpreting those patterns such as Joseph Campbell's *The*

Hero with a Thousand Faces, Bollingen Series, XVII (New York: Pantheon Books, 1949).

[6] It is interesting to note, however, that even in *The Divine Comedy* some attention to the initiatory aspects of the journey might be profitable. Dante criticism and scholarship has, in devoting itself to an analysis of the journey, neglected the character of the journeyer. Even so eminent a Dante authority as Karl Vossler states that "the poet has set forth his personality for us monumentally, statically; he has not developed it dynamically" (*Medieval Culture*, II, 216). It is good to see that Francis Fergusson's study of the *Purgatorio, Dante's Drama of the Mind* (Princeton: Princeton University Press, 1953), treats the development of the hero's character and perception in the second division of the work.

THE FIRST KNIGHTS

[1] *The Works of Sir Thomas Malory*, ed. Eugène Vinaver, 3 vols. paged consecutively (Oxford: Clarendon Press, 1947), pp. 119-20.

[2] *Chivalry*, ed. Edgar Prestage (London: Kegan, Paul, 1928), p. 5.

[3] See Maurice Valency, *In Praise of Love* (New York: Macmillan, 1958), p. 50.

[4] R. L. Kilgour, *The Decline of Chivalry as Shown in the French Literature of the late Middle Ages* (Cambridge, Mass.: Harvard University Press, 1937), xi. The introduction to Kilgour's book is the best, condensed treatment of the growth of chivalry I have seen.

[5] Valency, p. 41.

[6] Sidney Painter, *French Chivalry* (Ithaca, N. Y.: Cornell University Press, 1940) contains in its second chapter, "Feudal Chivalry," an extended discussion of the chivalric virtues.

[7] *Ibid.*, p. 2.

[8] *The Anglo-Saxon Chronicle*, Everyman's Library (London: J. M. Dent, 1912), p. 334.

[9] Valency, p. 41.

[10] *The Allegory of Love* (London: Oxford University Press, 1936), p. 2.

[11] I am acquainted with the argument, most vehemently expressed, I think, by Valency (p. 35) that courtly love was merely a literary convention, never a reality of social life, that "the eleventh century . . . did not invent the romantic passion; but it made it fashionable. The troubadours did not present the world with a new emotion; they established a literary genre."

[12] Lewis, pp. 6 ff.

[13] Painter (pp. 95 ff.) paints a striking picture of the place of women in medieval society.

[14] Valency (pp. 83 ff.) sees in this desire to "commit the ultimate disloyalty" evidence of the decline of feudalism.

[15] Painter, after a long discussion, concludes that courtly love had little real effect on the morality of the French nobility in the late Middle Ages and that while *fin amor* may have increased the amount of flirtation indulged in by the nobility, it did not increase adultery. But Painter himself clearly brands his conclusion as conjecture, and indeed it would seem to be based more on Painter's ideas of psychology than on any actual evidence of medieval practices. Margaret Adlum Gist, on the other hand, maintains (*Love and War in the English Medieval Romances* [Philadelphia: University of Pennsylvania Press, 1947], p. 193) that "in indicating the prevalance of adultery—of voluntary irregular unions—the romances, though they may exaggerate, are essentially truthful."

[16] Quoted by Sidney Painter, p. 113.

[17] E. A. Robinson, "Ben Jonson Entertains a Man from Stratford."

[18] I am deliberately excluding for the moment the *chansons de geste*, since the forms and values and probable origins of that genre make it a special case.

[19] *La Chanson de Roland*, l. 1138.

[20] *Malory*, p. 88.

[21] Not, please note, in terms of whether or not it makes use of courtly love or of any of the usual social trappings of the hero of romance.

[22] *La Chanson de Roland*, l. 1015.

THE USES OF LOVE

[1] Chrétien de Troyes, "Yvain," tr. W. W. Comfort, *Arthurian Romances*, Everyman's Library (London: J. M. Dent, 1914), p. 182. All passages from *Yvain* and from *Erec et Enide* quoted in my text are taken from this edition.

[2] *Epic and Romance* (New York: Dover Publications, 1957), p. 4.

[3] Simple at least in theory, if not always in practice. One must remember the tragic opposition of Garulf and Guthlaf, son and father, in the *Finnsburgh Fragment*, the tortured conflicts of the narrator of *The Wanderer*, and the cowardice of Beowulf's retainers.

[4] I am using the term "heroic age," as does Ker in *Epic and Romance*, in opposition to the "age of romance" or "age of chivalry" which followed in western Europe. Whether or not such periods actually existed is of little importance (cf. C. M. Bowra, *Heroic Poetry* [London: Macmillan, 1961]); as Bowra says (p. 29), "the truth is that composers of heroic poetry are not interested in chronology. . . . So far as they have a conception of a heroic age, it is artistic."

[5] "The Plot Structure in Four Romances of Chrétien de Troyes," *Studies in Philology*, L (1953), 4. Sarah F. Barrow, in *The Medieval Society Romances* (New York: Columbia University Press, 1944), suggests (pp. 64 ff.) that this double structure is the usual form of the romance, but her subsequent discussion shows clearly that it is actually seldom followed. Frappier, on the other hand, maintains that the structure of both *Erec* and *Yvain* is tripartite—the adventures culminating in the marriage of the lovers, their separation and trials, and their final reconciliation (*Arthurian Literature in the Middle Ages* [Oxford: Clarendon Press, 1959] p. 167). This "triptych" division, however, seems to me to ignore the fact that the second section of the poem is in fact a new beginning to the action, while the third is simply a continuation of and conclusion to the second.

[6] In *The Hero with a Thousand Faces*, Bollingen Series, XVII (New York: Pantheon Books, 1949).

[7] In *The King and the Corpse*, Bollingen Series, XI (New York: Pantheon Books, 1948).

[8] Campbell, pp. 245-46.

[9] A *Study of History*, abr. D. C. Somervell (New York: Oxford University Press, 1947), p. 63.

[10] Mircea Eliade, *Cosmos and History* (New York: Harper and Row, 1959), pp. 5-6.

[11] *Ibid.*

[12] Campbell, p. 193.

[13] Toynbee, p. 217.

[14] Campbell, p. 246.

[15] *Ibid.*, p. 218.

[16] Woods, p. 8.

[17] I cannot accept Jean Frappier's explanation (p. 170) that the "discord which separates them arises from the logic of their personalities."

[18] *Ibid.*, p. 167.

[19] "The Role of the Lion in Chrétien de Troyes' *Yvain*," *PMLA*, LXIV (1949), pp. 1143-44.

[20] .Woods, p. 10.

[21] *Ibid.*, p. 11.

[22] Professor Harris sees, rightly I think, Yvain's lion, his companion and aid, as a specifically Christian symbol.

[23] Harris, p. 1163.

[24] I am following here the standard relative chronology, which places the major romances of Chrétien in the following order: *Erec et Enide, Cliges, Lancelot, Yvain, Guillaume d'Angleterre, Perceval.*

[25] Frappier, p. 161.

[26] In the introduction to the "large" edition of *Cliges* (Halle: M. Niemeyer, 1910), vi ff.

[27] *The Evolution of the Arthurian Romances from the Beginnings down to the Year 1300*, 2 vols. (Baltimore: Johns Hopkins Press, 1923), I, 119.

[28] Frappier, p. 174.

[29] In *The King and the Corpse.*

[30] The last thousand lines of the poem were written by Godefroi de Lagny.

[31] Howard Patch, *The Other World, According to Descriptions in Medieval Literature* (Cambridge, Mass.: Harvard University Press, 1950).

[32] Bruce, II, 60.

THE STAINED KNIGHT

[1] Cf. the premarital relations of the lovers in *Escoufle* and *Partonopeus*. G. G. Coulton states that "the large majority of medieval romances . . . celebrate illicit love" (*Chaucer and His England* (London: Methuen, 1950), p. 201.

[2] "Marriage and *Amour Courtois* in Late Fourteenth-century England," *Essays presented to Charles Williams* (Oxford: Clarendon Press, 1947), p. 131.

[3] Maurice Valency, *In Praise of Love* (New York: Macmillan, 1958), p. 52.

[4] Alan M. Markman, "The Meaning of *Sir Gawain and the Green Knight*," PMLA, LXXII (1957), 575.

[5] Richard Hamilton Green, "Gawain's Shield and the Quest for Perfection," *ELH*, XIX (1962), 138.

[6] In *The King and the Corpse*, Bollingen Series, XI (New York: Pantheon Books, 1948).

[7] In "Sir Gawain and the Green Knight," *Scrutiny*, XVI (1949), 274-300.

[8] For a full presentation of the present state of the scholarship devoted to the poem, see Morton W. Bloomfield, "*Sir Gawain and the Green Knight*: An Appraisal," *PMLA*, LXXVI (1961), 7-19.

[9] *Les Rites de Passage* (Paris: E. Nourry, 1909), Chapter III.

[10] *The Hero with a Thousand Faces*, Bollingen Series, XVII (New York: Pantheon Books, 1949), pp. 49-59.

[11] Mircea Eliade, *Cosmos and Reality* (New York: Harper and Row, 1959), p. 54.

[12] *Ibid.*

[13] *Ibid.*, p. 69.

[14] "The Role of Morgan le Fay in *Sir Gawain and the Green Knight*," *ELH*, XVII (1960), 241-51. It is possible to object to this general line of argument by pointing out that this sort of religious imagery is usual in the medieval romance. However, *Sir Gawain and the Green Knight* is in structure, tone, and imagery far more tightly constructed than the usual romance, so tightly constructed in fact that it would be dangerous to pass off any one of the poem's myriad details as "merely" traditional. What is most apparent in *Sir Gawain and the Green Knight*, even upon the most cursory reading,

is that here, as in Chaucer, merely traditional elements become meaningful and functional when set by the author in the new context of the poem. The modesty prologue with which Chaucer's Franklin introduces his Breton lay was surely a piece of the medieval writer's standard story-telling equipment. Yet Chaucer uses this conventional device to throw light upon the dramatic role of the Franklin. So here, the Gawain poet adapts the conventional and largely meaningless religious imagery of the chivalric quest to his own purposes in defining the truly religious nature of Gawain's journey. It seems clear to me also that despite Speirs, Loomis, Weston, *et al.* to the contrary, the Gawain poet is a Christian writer, not a Druid in disguise. There is nothing in the poem, aside from the hero pattern which is universal and thus Christian as well as Celtic, which the poet could not have taken directly from the Christian tradition.

[15] *Sir Gawain and the Green Knight*, tr. Theodore Banks, Jr. (New York: F. S. Crofts and Co., Inc., 1929). All line references in my text are to Banks' translation.

[16] The general strain of religious imagery which runs throughout the poem reinforces this interpretation of the spiritual nature of Gawain's quest. Mass is heard daily in the castles of both Arthur and Bercilak. Gawain calls upon God to aid him in undertaking the quest (549). Arthur's court commends Gawain to God's protection on his departure (596), and Gawain, having thanked "Jesus and Julian" for his safe arrival at Bercilak's castle (774), blesses the porter who welcomes him there (839). Gawain is said to be the comeliest knight that Christ ever made (869). Bercilak's court rejoices that God has sent Gawain to them to be a model of courtly behavior (920-27). Gawain commends Bercilak to God's grace (1036-37). The interviews with Bercilak's lady are filled with oaths and commendations to Christ. Upon leaving, Gawain commends Bercilak's castle to Christ (2067) and blesses and is blessed by the porter of Bercilak's castle (2071-73). Bercilak and Gawain, after the conclusion of the beheading game, "each other commend / To the Prince of Paradise" (2472-73).

[17] The comparison of Bercilak's Lady to Guinevere affords a striking example of the *Gawain*-poet's functional use of conventional material. Although "fairer than Guinevere" is

a perfectly standard compliment in the medieval romance, used here in the midst of a comparison of the two courts and in a context involving an actual comparison involving the queen, the phrase surely constitutes more than a traditional compliment to the Lady. The obvious punning may represent the poet's way of calling special attention to the phrase.

[18] It is almost certain that he did. See J. R. Hulbert, "The Name of the Green Knight" (*Manly Anniversary Studies in Language and Literature* [Chicago, 1923], pp. 12-19) which demonstrates the *Gawain*-poet's knowledge of the Vulgate Cycle.

[19] The reason for Morgan's action is not given in the poem. Most scholars agree that Morgan's action stems from her traditional hatred of Guinevere (see G. L. Kittredge, *A Study of Sir Gawain and the Green Knight* [Cambridge, Mass.: Harvard University Press, 1916], p. 132) and that the introduction of Morgan into the poem represents a last minute attempt to supply Bercilak with some sort of motivation for initiating the game. John Speirs calls Bercilak's explanation a "bone for the rationalizing mind to play with. . . ." J. R. Hulbert states that Bercilak's explanation is "inherently unreasonable" ("Gawain and the Green Knight," *MP*, XIII [1915-16], 454). Kittredge (p. 132) suggests the explanation which I have adopted and modified here, that the poet was influenced "by that form of the tale of the Magic Horn [from which only the faithful woman might drink] which represents Morgan as sending the talisman to the court with the design of revealing Guinevere's unfaithfulness."

[20] Kittredge, pp. 129-30.
[21] *Ibid.*, p. 118.
[22] *Ibid.*

THE PHILOSOPHICAL KNIGHT

[1] *Chivalry*, ed. Edgar Prestage (London: Kegan, Paul, 1928), p. 37.
[2] *Ibid.*
[3] Particularly R. L. Kilgour in *The Decline of Chivalry as*

Shown in the French Literature of the Late Middle Ages
(Cambridge, Mass.: Harvard University Press, 1937).

[4] Kilgour, p. 418.

[5] *The Complete Works of Geoffrey Chaucer*, ed. F. N.
Robinson (Boston: Houghton, Mifflin, 1957), p. 271. The
line numbers in my text refer always to Robinson's edition.

[6] G. L. Kittredge, *Chaucer and His Poetry* (Cambridge,
Mass.: Harvard University Press, 1939), p. 48.

[7] *Ibid.*, p. 63.

[8] Both views are summarized in Robinson's notes, p. 632.

[9] *A Commentary on the General Prologue to the Canterbury Tales* (New York: Macmillan, 1948), p. 47.

[10] *Of Sondry Folk* (Austin: University of Texas Press,
1955), p. 33.

[11] A. R. Myers, *England in the Late Middle Ages*, Pelican
History of England (Harmondsworth, Middlesex: Penguin
Books, 1952), xiii.

[12] *Ibid.*, p. 52.

[13] Ralph Baldwin, "The Unity of the Canterbury Tales,"
Anglistica (Copenhagen: Rosenkilde and Bagger, 1955),
p. 84.

[14] See the lively debate between E. Talbot Donaldson
and R. E. Kaske in *Critical Approaches to Medieval Literature*, English Institute Essays, 1958-59 (New York: Columbia
University Press, 1960), pp. 1-60.

[15] Most notably by D. W. Robertson, Jr., and Bernard
F. Huppe in *Piers Plowman and Scriptural Tradition* (Princeton: Princeton University Press, 1951).

[16] Baldwin, p. 92.

[17] *Ibid.*, p. 86.

[18] *Ibid.*, p. 92.

[19] *Ibid.*, p. 90.

[20] See R. M. Lumiansky, "The Degree of Completeness of
The Canterbury Tales," *Tulane Studies in English*, VI
(1956), 5-13.

[21] See Lumiansky, *Of Sondry Folk, passim.*

[22] Baldwin, p. 92.

[23] *A Study of History*, abr. D. C. Somervell (London: Oxford University Press, 1947), p. 217.

[24] I am inclined to think that the Host's stated intention

of having each pilgrim tell four stories on the journey is meant by Chaucer as a device to expose Harry Bailly's pretentiousness, but that there is no doubt at all that he meant to return the pilgrimage to London.

[25] Arthur W. Hoffman, "Chaucer's Prologue to Pilgrimage: The Two Voices," *ELH*, **XXI** (1954), 3.

[26] Kittredge, pp. 185 ff.

[27] For example, by Arthur B. Ferguson, *The Indian Summer of English Chivalry* (Durham: Duke University Press, 1960), p. 223.

[28] *Of Sondry Folk*, pp. 29-49.

[29] It seems clear that a version of the *Knight's Tale* was composed by Chaucer in the early 1380's at about the time he was working on *Troilus and Criseyde*.

[30] See J. P. Roppolo, "The Converted Knight in Chaucer's *Wife of Bath's Tale*," *College English*, XII (1951), 263-69.

[31] Lumiansky, *Of Sondry Folk*, pp. 181-93.

THE TRAGIC KNIGHT

[1] Arthur B. Ferguson, *The Indian Summer of English Chivalry* (Durham: Duke University Press, 1960), xiv.

[2] *Ibid.*, p. 6.

[3] Cf. *ibid.*, pp. 104 ff.

[4] *Ibid.*, p. 107.

[5] E. Talbot Donaldson, *Piers Plowman: The C-Text and Its Poet* (New Haven: Yale University Press, 1949), p. 92.

[6] Ferguson, p. 106.

[7] *The Boke of the Ordre of Chyvalry*, ed. A. T. P. Byles, Early English Text Society, o.s. 40 (London: Oxford University Press, 1926), pp. 122-23.

[8] *The Works of Sir Thomas Malory*, ed. Eugène Vinaver, 3 vols. paged consecutively (Oxford: Clarendon Press, 1947), p. 120. This didactic point of view toward Malory's work is thoroughly explored by Ferguson (p. 42 ff.).

[9] Ferguson, p. 47.

[10] I realize that Malory's biography (and almost certainly the author of the *Morte Darthur* and the criminal knight of Newbold Revell are one and the same man) would hardly

lead one to think that he held strongly any notions of knightly propriety. Yet as C. S. Lewis points out ("The English Prose *Morte*," *Essays on Malory* [Oxford: Clarendon Press, 1963], pp. 9-10), the *Morte Darthur* undeniably demonstrates "an unforced reverence not only for courage . . . but for mercy, humility, graciousness, and good faith," and it may well be that the legal charges against Malory are exaggerated. "He might," says Lewis, "on the evidence, have been as good a knight as Tristram; for what should we think of Tristram himself if our knowledge of him were derived only from King Mark's solicitors?"

[11] Vinaver, p. lxv.

[12] Though more of Dinadan actually remains in Malory than is commonly imagined.

[13] Vinaver, lxxxii.

[14] P. E. Tucker, "Chivalry in the Morte," *Essays on Malory*, pp. 64-103.

[15] Ferguson, p. 54.

[16] *Ibid.*

[17] Cf. R. H. Wilson, "Malory's Early Knowledge of Arthurian Romance," *University of Texas Studies in English*, XXX (1951), 1-23.

[18] Ferguson, p. 42.

[19] Cf. Vinaver's statement (1606) that "how little he [Malory] made . . . of the Wheel of Fortune will be seen from his treatment of two of the most important passages in his French source."

[20] Vinaver, p. 1607.

[21] *Arthurian Torso* (London: Oxford University Press, 1948), p. 200.

[22] Above, p. 40.

[23] "The Archetypes of Literature," *Kenyon Review*, XIII (1951), 107. Interestingly enough, the failure of John Speir's much discussed attempt to present *Sir Gawain and the Green Knight* in mythic terms (*Scrutiny*, XVI [1949], 274-300) may be due to the fact that he in fact identifies *Sir Gawain and the Green Knight* as a "dawn, spring, and birth" myth, when it actually reflects the failure rather than the success of the hero.

[24] Frye, p. 104.

THE ALLEGORICAL KNIGHT

[1] *The Scholemaster*, ed. W. A. Wright (Cambridge: Cambridge University Press, 1904), pp. 230-31.

[2] Arthur B. Ferguson, *The Indian Summer of English Chivalry* (Durham: Duke University Press, 1960), p. 98.

[3] The phrase is Edwin Greenlaw's ("Materials for the Study of the English Renaissance," *Modern Language Notes*, XLII [1927], 183).

[4] E. A. Greenlaw, *Studies in Spenser's Historical Allegory* (Baltimore: Johns Hopkins Press, 1932), p. 54.

[5] Ferguson, p. 94.

[6] For a thorough discussion of Arthurian celebrations in Tudor times, see Charles Bowie Millican, *Spenser and the Table Round* (Cambridge, Mass.: Harvard University Press, 1932), pp. 54 ff.

[7] Ferguson, p. 68.

[8] *The Pastime of Pleasure*, ed. W. E. Mead, Early English Text Society, o.s. 173 (London: Oxford University Press, 1928), pp. 285-86.

[9] *Ibid.*, xix.

[10] Ferguson, p. 65.

[11] Cf. Mead, xlv, n. 3.

[12] Cf. my "Courtly Love in Malory," *ELH*, XXVII (1960), 163-76.

[13] Ferguson, p. 94.

[14] *Ibid.*, p. 97.

[15] The fact that Malory's influence on Spenser is negligible is itself of great interest and significance. C. S. Lewis's statement (*The Allegory of Love* [London: Oxford University Press, 1936], p. 305) that he should be hard put to show by internal evidence that Spenser had read much of Malory is no real exaggeration. As Greenlaw remarks, "Malory [in Spenser's age] was read, but except for a few insignificant romances was not imitated" (*Studies in Spenser's Historical Allegory*, p. 51).

[16] E. M. W. Tillyard, *The English Epic and Its Background* (London: Chatto and Windus, 1954), p. 176.

[17] Lewis, p. 306.

[18] Graham Hough, *A Preface to the Faerie Queene* (New York: W. W. Norton, 1963), p. 170.

[19] "Introduction" to *The Poetical Works of Edmund Spenser*, Oxford Standard Authors Series (London: Oxford University Press, 1912), xli. All line references in my text are to this edition.

[20] E. A. Greenlaw, "The Faerie Queene," *Encyclopaedia Americana*.

[21] Hough, pp. 139-40.

[22] Lewis, p. 302.

[23] E. A. Greenlaw and others, *The Works of Edmund Spenser: A Variorum Edition*, 7 vols. (Baltimore: Johns Hopkins Press, 1932-38), I, 247.

[24] Greenlaw states (Review of Herbert E. Cory's *Edmund Spenser, A Critical Study, Modern Language Notes*, XXXV [1920], 170) that Spenser "following the later Arthurian romances uses romance situations as *symbols* of spiritual matters." However, such symbolic uses are so rare in the romance before Spenser, except, of course, in the various Grail romances, that their influence on Spenser must be considered negligible, if indeed it is present at all. The consistently and abstractly allegorical knight is almost totally an invention of Spenser's.

[25] "Remarks on the Fairy Queen," *The Works of Spenser*, 6 vols. (London: J. and R. Tonson and S. Draper, 1750), I, lxi.

[26] "Spenser's Imitations from Ariosto," *PMLA*, XXII (1897), 190 ff.

[27] See Marie Walther, *Malory's Einfluss auf Spenser's Faerie Queene* (Eisleben, 1898) and Edmund Kemper Broadus, "The Red Cross Knight and *Lybeaus Desconus*," *Modern Language Notes*, XVIII (1903), 202-204.

[28] By Padelford in the *Variorum Spenser*, p. 394.

[29] *Spenser's Faerie Queene: An Interpretation* (London: Edward Arnold and Company, 1934), p. 6.

[30] The reader is directed to the excellent discussion of love in Spenser contained in Chapter VIII of Leicester Bradner's *Edmund Spenser and The Faerie Queene* (Chicago: University of Chicago Press, 1948).

[31] There is some evidence in the *Morte Darthur* that Malory was strongly opposed to courtly love because of its debilitative effects on chivalry and on knighthood (see my "Courtly Love in Malory").

[32] Lewis, pp. 338 ff.

[33] Hough, p. 231.

[34] *Chivalry in English Literature* (Cambridge, Mass.: Harvard University Press, 1912), p. 164.

[35] Spenser himself spent two years in pastoral retirement at Wilton.

[36] See Schofield for just such a listing and discussion.

THE LAST KNIGHTS

[1] I do not believe there to be any direct relationship here in spite of Schofield's statement that Shakespeare "must have been strongly drawn" to Sir Dagonet and, especially, Sir Dinadan (*Chivalry in English Literature* [Cambridge, Mass.: Harvard University Press, 1912], p. 220).

[2] *The Indian Summer of English Chivalry* (Durham: Duke University Press, 1960), p. 226.

[3] Quoted by Schofield (pp. 216-17) from Caxton's translation of *The Order of Chivalry*.

[4] See R. L. Kilgour, *The Decline of Chivalry as Shown in the French Literature of the Late Middle Ages* (Cambridge, Mass.: Harvard University Press, 1937), p. 419.

[5] Ferguson, p. 223.

[6] *Ibid.*, pp. 225-26.

[7] Hallett Smith, *Elizabethan Poetry* (Cambridge, Mass.: Harvard University Press, 1952), pp. 138-39.

[8] *Ibid.*, pp. 141-42.

[9] *The Arthurian Legend in the Seventeenth Century* (Baltimore: Johns Hopkins Press, 1932), vii.

[10] Dryden's opera *King Arthur* makes no use of the traditional Arthur story.

[11] *English Literature in the Earlier Seventeenth Century* (London: Oxford University Press, 1962), p. 222.

[12] For a thorough discussion of Milton's projected use of the legend, see Brinkley, pp. 126-41.

[13] Mircea Eliade, *Cosmos and History* (New York: Harper and Row, 1959), p. 37.

INDEX